"Accepting your worth is the first
step to realization."

The circled dot is an ancient sacred symbol that re-minds us to embrace our true essence. The dot represents our soul-self, and the circle our expression into reality.

Take time to reflect on this symbol. Understanding its meaning can profoundly deepen your connection to yourself and the world around you.

Nancy DeYoung

I MATTER
by Nancy DeYoung

ISBN 978-0-9844103-9-2
Printed in the United States of America

Contents

Chapter 1
Self-Worth

*If you know your true worth, you don't
need anyone to confirm it.*

Alan Cohen

Each person's unique existence holds value. We
all have an impact on the world, no matter how big or
small. I Matter is an empowering realization that can
transform how we perceive ourselves and interact with
life. Knowing our value makes us more confident and
likely to live our dreams with a strong purpose and
motivation.

I hadn't thought much about mattering until
Adamus St. Germain, channeled by Geoffrey Hoppe,
asked what mattered in one of his talks. That question
started me on a quest. It seemed like a simple enough
inquiry, and I listed many things I deemed important.
However, upon deeper reflection, I realized that the
items on my list were fleeting and ultimately insignificant.

In the grand scheme—whether in a day, a month,
five years, or ten thousand years—their relevance
would fade. The one constant that would endure

forever was ME. I realized that I am what matters. This is true for each of us, which also makes YOU the most important consideration in your world. Why did I not know that? Did other people know they matter?

I wanted to know more. What did science have to say about the matter of mattering? Besides defining matter as any substance that has mass and occupies space, it didn't offer much. Yet, the word 'matter' has many applications, including phrases like "What's the matter?" "As a matter of fact," "It's no laughing matter," and "It's a matter of time."

For our purposes, I Matter means that my existence has value. I Matter implies that I love myself enough to maintain my body, mind, and emotions in a healthy state so I can contribute positively to the world, form meaningful relationships, and pursue my passions and dreams. By the mere fact that I exist, I deserve my place in the world.

I Matter transcends a mere affirmation; it is a profound acknowledgment of our intrinsic worth, dignity, and potential. So, the next time you question your significance, remember the truth in these two simple words: I Matter.

Know Your Worth

Self-worth is fundamental in knowing we matter; it profoundly influences our perception of who we are and how much we love ourselves. To fully grasp our value, we must release all barriers, especially the long-held beliefs that suggest we are undeserving and must prove our right to exist.

Growing up, many of us were conditioned to accept a reality where we constantly had to prove our worth and follow the rules. If we didn't, there were consequences, usually physical punishment or loss of love and respect. We learned to silence our true selves to avoid rocking the boat. The narrative told us that good things are rare and that hard work is the key to success. It assured us that suffering would bring rewards later, usually in the afterlife.

For many, life has taught that "the world is not safe," "money doesn't grow on trees," "good things never last," and "you can't make a living as an artist." Of course, there are exceptions, but even those who grow up in a loving environment are subjected to limiting beliefs. This programming shapes our lives by trapping us in a mindset that restricts our potential.

The widespread use of guilt is a common theme in our society. This programming comes from well-meaning individuals who believe they are teaching discipline, as well as from those with questionable intentions, such as authority figures seeking to maintain control. The program is typically enforced through the use of punishment and reward, creating an ongoing cycle of fear and compliance. If we accept and internalize these messages, our self-worth is affected, making us feel as though we have no voice or control over our lives.

The truth is, self-worth does not need to be earned or validated. It's not dependent on external achievements, career success, public recognition, or material possessions, which are temporary and often tied to societal approval. Instead, self-worth comes from an inner acknowledgment of one's inherent value as a human being. Recognizing this fosters a sense of inner peace and confidence.

Years ago, in one of Stuart Wilde's lectures, he had this to say.

People have always atoned for their sins by giving their crops and animals to the temple in what were called 'offerings.' These offerings, of course, supported the clergy. When the people were being good, the donations dropped off, so the priests devised a new plan. They claimed people were born in sin, and they needed to be absolved of that sin, or they would go to hell. They called this 'original sin.' The people could be saved by giving more offerings to the temple. Stuart said the priests created original sin because they had to keep the goats coming around to the temple, and they called it 'original' because it was a "damn clever idea!"

How many of our beliefs were born out of filling someone else's needs?

We are told that we are unworthy and inherently bad, and these destructive notions have become deeply ingrained in us. We rarely question the origins of this programming or who benefits from it, allowing the puppet masters to keep us obedient to their will.

Guilt is a powerful tool that often gets us to do what others want. It has long played a role in controlling people and has deprived us of knowing our divinity. We are put down and diminished daily by bosses, family, teachers, friends, and officials. Depending on the controller's skill, this may be obvious or subtle. After lifetimes of conditioning, it is a wonder we have any remaining dignity or self-awareness.

The idea that we have to earn our worthiness is ludicrous! This could not be further from the truth. It is unfathomable how the divine light beings we are could ever entertain such a crazy notion. We are not sinners. We are here to have experiences—all kinds of experiences. The truth is that self-worth is self-worth; it is that simple. By the very fact that we exist, we are valuable and precious.

> *I will never yield my worth.*
>
> Jasmine Crockett

When we truly recognize our worth and know that we matter, we unlock a profound sense of joy that radiates from within. This awareness opens us to accept and celebrate our unique qualities, acknowledging that they contribute to our individuality. We learn to embrace our imperfections, seeing them not as flaws but as integral parts of our human experience that foster growth and resilience. We gain the confidence to be all that we can be, knowing that we play a valuable role in the tapestry of life.

In a world that emphasizes external validation and comparison, embracing the notion that I Matter is a radical act of self-acceptance and empowerment.

Leaders who seek to control and manipulate people do not find this beneficial to their agenda.

The credit for the following quote is attributed to George Orwell's *1984*, but it is also associated with Machiavelli.

> *The first rule of 'statecraft' is to keep the people in a state of ignorance and fear. Don't let them get a whiff of their own potential power. Because if they do, we're all goners!*

The puppet masters, often powerful elites or influential groups, manipulate public perceptions and narratives to create a convincing illusion that individuals lack the knowledge and ability to govern themselves. They achieve this by spreading fear and uncertainty, leading people to believe that without their leadership, chaos and danger will ensue. This fear is often reinforced through media portrayals and political rhetoric.

As a result, many people willingly give up control and delegate their rights to a person or organization, believing it will provide security and stability. However, in doing so, they relinquish not only their autonomy but also their fundamental freedom to self-govern and make informed decisions about their own lives and communities. This fosters dependency on authority figures and perpetuates a cycle of control and submission.

When we give authority to a person or a group, we relinquish our freedom to self-govern.

When you trade liberty for security, you end up with neither.

Benjamin Franklin

We all have difficulty accepting our worth to some degree, but one group that has a particularly hard time is those who have dedicated their lives to caring for others. These individuals pour so much of themselves into others that the idea of prioritizing their own needs seems selfish.

Accepting their worthiness and receiving help from others does not feel possible for them. Often, they can only accept support when they are completely worn down and have no other choice. This situation frequently applies to healthcare professionals, teachers, social workers, and employees who are always at their supervisor's beck and call.

These caretakers have their reasons for what they do, and one worth examining is whether, by giving so much to others, they might also be controlling the narrative. Regardless of their intentions, the depletion they feel can lead to burnout and an inability to continue their work. They need to prioritize and understand that self-care is not a selfish luxury, but a necessary step to enable them to thrive and continue sharing their unique gifts.

We can't be too busy to stop for gas!

You Matter

At some point in life, many of us grapple with self-doubt, questioning our significance and wondering if we truly matter. We ask ourselves why we are here and whether anyone cares. Valuing oneself is not something our culture typically promotes. Instead, it seems to do everything to discourage it.

Clear your mind, look in the mirror, and tell yourself, "I Matter." How did that feel? Was it sincere? If you answered yes, ask yourself who you matter to. If you cannot think of one person other than yourself, that may be a heartbreaking realization, but in the end, it doesn't matter what anyone else thinks. All that matters is that you accept the truth of your being: I Matter, and I Am that I Am.

Custer Crossing South Dakota

Many people find it easier to tell another person they matter than to accept their own worthiness. Think of someone you care about and say, "You Matter." Was telling another easier than telling yourself? If you physically told someone, were they able to accept it, or did they shrug it off?

When we feel unworthy, we doubt ourselves and hesitate to take action. If we believe we don't matter or make a difference, it is easy to back away from action and fail to realize our purpose. Acknowledging our value makes us more likely to set healthy boundaries, pursue our goals, and advocate for our needs. It is a guiding principle for making choices that align with our true nature. As we cultivate self-love, our inner light shines brightly, positively impacting not only ourselves but also those around us.

Passion

The word 'passion' can bring up different things. The suffering of Jesus. Strong emotion. One's work. Hallmark movies. Love affairs. It is used in many contexts, but here, we will look at passion as a by-product of the soul's joy of being in existence.

When we experience this profound joy, we may feel the urge to pause and fully immerse ourselves in the bliss. Alternatively, we may want to jump up and take immediate action. Whatever we choose, we'll have the energy and enthusiasm for it. Tapping into this joy once will get us started, but we must return to that space periodically to maintain the momentum and keep the creative flow alive.

What once allowed you to feel your joy may change after you awaken to your true nature as an embodied master. During this transition, you may feel you are living in a void. Feeling lost is not a setback; it's a signal that you are transforming, and so are your priorities. This new approach to life is unfamiliar, so it feels strange and unreliable. However, in time, you will see that this is how life was meant to be; it opens the door to extraordinary magic and unlimited possibilities. Embrace the journey; it is where true fulfillment lies.

Passion can fade if we have achieved everything we want in this world, but as long as we are here, there is something left to be gained, or we wouldn't be here. The challenge is to think creatively and discover what interests us. Then do it!

Immersing yourself in a project can be beneficial. Consider learning another language, making a fairy house, writing your memoir, birdwatching, spending time with children, visiting new places, planting flowers, organizing your closets, building a new shed, experimenting with recipes, or hiking while learning about the area's plants and minerals. Many activities offer a compelling opportunity to enrich your life and broaden your horizons. That said, it can also be a time of inner solace.

No Fear!

Along with guilt, fear is one of our greatest enemies. It destroys self-worth and keeps us from moving forward. So dream; dream as big as you can. If you can imagine it, it is a reality somewhere. However, some aspirations may not come to fruition, and it's important to understand why, so you don't doubt yourself.

This can occur if the goal is not aligned with your energy, the timing isn't quite right, or the outcome isn't the primary focus; the real treasure might lie in the journey itself. Or it could be a combination of these factors. But you will never know if you don't dream the dream and go for it.

Sometimes, there is a need to shift our energy to help us reach our goal.

I was hiking the Red Hills in California on a hot day. I had been there before, but on this day, I decided to take a different trail. After walking up and down the hills for hours, my heart was pounding, my muscles were complaining, my body was overheated, and my face felt on fire. My water was dangerously low. The more my body hurt, the more my brain tried to convince me I was going to have a heart attack. I rested a few times, but it didn't help. Then I realized my focus was on how bad I felt, not the beauty around me, which was difficult considering the rocky trail.

I reined in my fear and exhaustion and began feeling my body taking in life force with each breath. I walked more slowly so I could enjoy the surrounding mountains. Before long, my respiration slowed, and I felt I could finish the hike without calling 9-1-1. When I let go of fear, my body was able to do what it needed. I was quite

pleased and extremely relieved when I made it
back to the car.

By confronting issues within ourselves, we transform our external reality.

Pixabay.com

Releasing fear allows energy to flow. No Fear!
This builds confidence, and our self-worth grows along
with the awareness that we matter.

Chapter 2
Just Experience

When you come to a fork in the road, take it.
Yogi Berra

People ask, "Why am I here?" and "What should I do with my life?" We all know why we are here, but we haven't been taught to trust our intuition. Instead, we often look to school counselors, adults with agendas, or friends for answers. They cannot give us the answers, especially as we approach our enlightenment. It can be confusing because we are releasing our old beliefs, but we may not consciously know what this new path looks like. But that's okay because we've never done this before; it unfolds as we go.

When I think about making sense of this topsy-turvy world, the song from the 1966 movie *Alfie* comes to mind, "What's it all about, Alfie?" One thing I can tell you is that life is about having experiences, and each one brings us closer to living as enlightened beings. Everything we do, think, and say contains wisdom that our master selves harvest.

In our quest for self-realization, we take on many lives and assume various roles. Sometimes, we repeat experiences out of habit, a desire to gain different perspectives, or for reasons known only to us. Ultimately, it's about loving ourselves and recognizing that we are worthy and that we matter.

Our birth into the human form is the most extreme event in our lives. To that, we add childhood illnesses, school stresses, and relationships with siblings, parents, friends, coworkers, and authority figures. Perhaps we join the military, which comes with its own set of challenges. We have hundreds of experiences every day. This world is a smorgasbord of possibilities, and we constantly make choices. Regardless of what we decide, each choice presents an opportunity to gather experience that our master selves distill into wisdom.

We have been doing this for a very long time, and the process is becoming wearisome. Now that we are awake, we may be ready to leave the human experience behind. But don't dismiss it too quickly. Use your time here to experience everything you have ever wanted while enjoying embodied mastery. It can be mystical and magical. Enjoy the journey because you may never pass this way again!

Since life is about having a wide range of experiences, it follows that we can never make a mistake. We label things as good, bad, right, and wrong due to our programming; however, they are just experiences.

I can hear you saying, "But! But! What about...?" Okay. I will quickly add that we make choices, and consequences follow. We may feel it was a huge mistake that we quit school and are now working at 'Wally World,' or that we ever started smoking and now have lung disease, or that we drove after drinking and got a ticket. It is easy to look at those things as mistakes, but were they? They could be the best things we ever did for ourselves! Even if we didn't see it then, there was some benefit, or we wouldn't have done it.

A young friend was driving drunk and tried to outrun the police. He stopped before anything happened and spent some time in jail. Being taken away from his wife and infant son showed him what he had to lose. Part of his probation was attending Alcoholics Anonymous (AA) meetings. Since he no longer had a license and couldn't drive, he joined a Narcotics Anonymous (NA) group near his home. He stopped drinking and, after some time, began leading the NA group. He would tell you that what had seemed so horrible was precisely what he needed to get his life on track.

Look at events without judgment and see what good came from your 'mistakes,' keeping in mind that you may not have completed the cycle. In the movie *The Best Exotic Marigold Hotel*, one of the characters said, "In India, we have the saying that everything will be all right in the end, so if it is not all right, it's not the end." It can take months or maybe years to see the bigger picture. So don't judge too quickly.

You may accept that your experiences have worked out for the best, but what about the 'horrible' things that happen to others? The same is true; everyone is on a path designed to provide the experiences and wisdom their souls seek.

We can make life easier by following one path over another, but there is always a reason for our choices. When my daughter was sixteen, she said, "Mom, I know you are right, but I have to do it my way." How could I argue with that? It seemed she was choosing the hard path, but she knew what she needed.

It was an early lesson for me that people must follow their own path, regardless of what I think. Just know that nothing happens to anyone except in accordance with their state of consciousness, which always brings them to their enlightenment.

If you are in a compromising situation, step back and consider your options. Though your mind may initially see none, the ideal solution will reveal itself if you connect with your serene inner space.

Doing nothing often leads to the very best
of something.

Winnie the Pooh
A.A. Milne

Entering that quiet space can be challenging, especially when emotional baggage weighs on us. We have to begin where we are, which means releasing the blockages we cling to. This process does not have to be complicated or painful; simply acknowledge them and give them to your master self when they arise. The master self will transform them into wisdom.

Supportive Alignments

Astrology is not my area of expertise, but it's hard to ignore how celestial alignments have shaped human history. At the time of Jesus, we left the Arian Age, which was characterized by the harsh notion of "an eye for an eye."

For the past 2,000 years, we have been navigating the Piscean Age, during which the mantra "He ain't heavy; he's my brother" prevailed. We have believed we were responsible for others and that it was our duty to bear their burdens. This mindset became ingrained in us, and we have embodied this programming for so long that we now struggle to shift our perspective to taking full responsibility for our own lives while allowing others to do the same.

The Piscean Age is coming to a close, giving way to the Aquarian Age. With this shift in energy comes the end of suffering and the need to be the savior. It's time for Jesus to come down from the cross, allowing us to release guilt, shame, and misguided beliefs. Once we stop beating ourselves, we may be better able to help others. The airlines have it right when they advise putting on our oxygen mask before assisting another.

Realizing you are a divine being may cause you to feel you are a superhero and that it is up to you to save the world. Is that true? Could you even if you tried? And does the world need or want to be saved— whatever that means? I'm not saying it's not true for you, but it is something to consider once you look at life outside your programs and belief systems.

An aspect of our human experience is giving joyful service, so I am not suggesting that we withhold support or deny help when we need it. We all can use a helping hand from time to time. However, when we focus on our obligations and define ourselves by our actions, we risk losing touch with our authentic selves. Immersing ourselves in others' dramas makes it challenging to live in the grace of I Matter.

As we move deeper into the Aquarian Age, everyone must take responsibility for themselves. Although people surround us, the path to sovereignty is a solitary journey that only we can navigate. However, our divine essence is always with us, providing guidance and unwavering support.

We are in the infancy of living as self-aware, self-directed beings. This is a whole new paradigm. We may feel a range of emotions, including fear, excitement, motivation, uncertainty, confidence, resistance, and inspiration, all at the same time. How can it be otherwise when we stand on the precipice, ready to fly?

Sense Perception

To have an abundance of experiences, we needed a vessel. We chose the human form, which includes the senses of touch, taste, smell, hearing, and sight. Without them, our ability to engage with the world would be severely compromised.

Some individuals have lived productive lives without one sense, but Helen Keller was exceptional in that she led a remarkable life without two primary senses: sight and hearing. While this was extremely difficult, living without three senses would decrease one's ability to interact with life to such an extent that the rationale for maintaining a physical body becomes questionable.

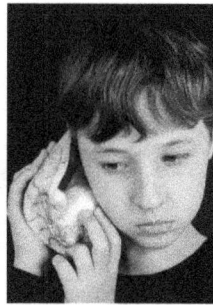

Sense of Hearing - Pixabay.com

As strange as it may sound, people sometimes willingly give up one of their senses. Perhaps the person wants to develop another sense more fully, or pain could be connected to the input.

I knew a man who had hearing loss. His wife was always complaining about something, and often, the subject of her complaint was him. Even after using ear-wax removal techniques, his ears were filled with wax. It appeared he grew tired of hearing her and repressed that sense. This is not to say he did this consciously, but it happened nonetheless.

Sense of Touch - Pixabay.com

Without a physical body and its senses, we cannot know what it is like to see a beautiful garden, smell soup simmering on a cold winter day, delight in the flavors of coffee or chocolate, hear the ebb and flow of a symphony, or feel the warm hug of a loved one. We require a human body with human senses to experience these sensations.

I did not recognize what a gift they were until I had the following experience; my friend showed this to me in a very visceral way.

Michael had died unexpectedly. Every time I passed his abandoned house, my attention was drawn to it, and I thought about him. One day, I was with a Native American friend when we drove by, and, in my head, I heard Michael scream at me to stop there. So we did. I tuned in to him and realized he wanted me to disassemble his medicine wheel, which my friend confirmed needed to be done if it wasn't being used. We took it apart stone by stone. She said the prayer ties he had placed there needed to be burned.[1] So I took them back to town.

She went home, and I again tuned in and asked Michael what he wanted me to do because I couldn't think of a place to light a fire. In my inner vision, he showed me the park by Canyon Lake, which has several fire pits. He was very specific about which one he wanted me to use. Since it was a holiday weekend, I figured someone would be using that shelter for a picnic, but I went anyway. To my surprise, no one was there. I lit the fire. The ties were dry tobacco and should have burned quickly, but they didn't; it took hours. I waited, and as the sun set, the fire finally died. The lake shimmered with gold and pink hues. It was a spectacular sight.

---

[1] Prayer ties are offerings made from squares of red, yellow, white, or black fabric that are folded and filled with tobacco as one prays. The ends are gathered, and the bundle is tied to a tree or string.

Michael was with me the whole time. As the fire burned, I felt him releasing the prayers he had placed in the ties. He then asked if he could enter my body to look out over the lake one last time through human eyes. I agreed, and after a few moments, he left. I have not felt his presence since then.

Sense of Sight - Canyon Lake SD

It was very unusual for me to allow him or any being to enter my body, but this felt right. It was the correct decision because I received a gift that would stay with me. I experienced the same wonder and awe he felt as he looked at the sun setting over the lake through my eyes. Until that moment, I had never fully appreciated the preciousness of the human senses.

We have pleasant experiences through our senses, and I won't deny that we also have ones that most humans would never consciously choose. Soul, on the other hand, is ecstatic for all of them. The soul does not label or judge things as good or bad—it is all just experience! We may say, "Easy for it to be so impartial since we, the humans, are the ones on the front line!" Then comes the day when we realize there is no separation between us and soul. We are soul!

Sense of Smell – AI Generated

Oil and Vinegar Therapy

How can we get into our natural state of well-being? Of course, the ideal is just to be it, but if you need help, consider this. I have tried many different ways, but the one I have had the most fun with is what I call 'Oil and Vinegar Therapy.'

While in South Dakota, a friend invited me to a brunch he had prepared for a small group of friends. The table was laden with a vast array of fresh fruit, berries, cheeses, meats, crackers, breads, different kinds of vinegar, and oils. They weren't just any vinegars or oils; they were the expensive flavored ones you purchase from the oil store. I dipped and swirled one of the delicacies in Tuscan Herb oil that he had paired with Black Mission Fig balsamic vinegar. That first bite was a total surprise! My taste buds danced; I was transported to a state of nirvana. I greedily tried all of the flavors and combinations.

Before I left town, we visited the oil store, and I selected four different kinds of vinegar and two oils; I also can't forget to mention the black truffle-infused salt. My upcoming move would be costly, but I knew I had to purchase some of these incredible treasures to take me out of the mundane world, should I get stuck.

The senses play a significant role in the human experience. We extensively use sight, sound, touch, and smell to monitor our surroundings. However, the sense of taste seems to be the one that is frequently overlooked. Sure, we eat, but how often do we pause to savor what we put in our mouths?

Exposing this sense to fantastic flavors can take us to new heights. I frequently use Oil and Vinegar

Therapy and have extended this appreciation to other foods. A side benefit is that I eat foods that are more supportive of my body, and if I splurge on less nutritious options, I savor every bite of them!

Sense of Taste - Pixabay.com

Many spiritual practices involve suffering and difficult-to-follow routines, but if you find something that is truly a taste sensation, it will be no problem. Take a bite and allow it to transport you to paradise. What will your Oil and Vinegar Therapy be? As you enjoy it, remind yourself, "I Matter."

Chapter 3
After Awakening

Change is not a threat; it's an opportunity.
Seth Godin

You've likely delved into your community and explored online resources to uncover the mysteries of the invisible world. Waking up can be challenging, and I suspect your journey was not without its trials. Your path is uniquely your own, shaped by your experiences and insights.

Perhaps, like me, you entered this life wide awake, but found that there were times when you had to go to sleep to survive. My father taught me this as an infant, and I often used that survival technique.

I heard crying. I stood up in my crib and looked out the bedroom doorway. I could see my mother and father. It was my mother sobbing. I started crying, and Dad came to me and sternly told me to stop it and go to sleep. He shut the door. I plopped down in my bed and did as I was told. I slipped out of my body and went to a place where I felt safe. I'm not sure where that was; it just wasn't 'here.'

Herman Melville described such a place as:
It's not down on any map; true places never are.

Moby Dick
Herman Melville

Despite this rocky start, I knew deep inside that this was my lifetime to realize my divinity. I couldn't have put it into words, but that inner knowing has been my guiding star. At times, I felt a panic that I wouldn't make it, but there was also a greater, soul-knowingness that this was the time, and nothing could interfere.

As I was waking up, I stated with full intent that I wanted whatever would help me, and I wanted it NOW. Things happened that cleared old programs and beliefs, but that did not happen overnight. After all, I had been accumulating them for lifetimes. Once the blocks cleared, it was safe to be in the body. Everything I needed to support me and my journey came with ease and grace; it often seemed like magic. I no longer needed to escape from anything; all was a treasured experience.

You, too, have come to realize that life is more than what you were told. Like Harry Potter, you have emerged from the cupboard under the stairs and are looking deeper into the secrets of life. You know what you have been taught is wrong or only part of the truth, and although you may not be able to define it, you feel it. However, it is easy to doubt yourself when the world says things and demonstrates behaviors that don't align with what you inherently know.

You know we must treat life, others, and the planet with respect. You see the imbalances that many people are oblivious to. You have lost interest in the mundane things that previously held your attention. If you experience stress, struggle, and a loss of hope, know that these feelings are not uncommon. You no longer live in a world of illusion; the blinders are off, and the truth is becoming your reality. At first, this may be confusing, but it will all make sense, so hang in there.

Medical or recreational drugs are tools some people use to get respite from the chaos they feel. They may provide relief for a while, but the inner gnawing remains when the effects wear off. You know there has to be another way, but what?

You encounter individuals who offer solutions. Sometimes, those solutions further their agenda and cause issues and entanglements you later have to clean up. Exercising discernment is vital.

Sonya was awake, and life made no sense. She saw things differently, and her family did not understand her. When she became suicidal, they had her placed on meds. To find people who understood her, she went online and found a group in Arizona. She began communicating with them and started feeling better about herself. She thought she had found her soul family. She stopped taking her meds, moved to Arizona, and joined the commune. She lived in the compound and participated in group activities, including the use of DMT (Dimethyltryptamine). This hallucinogen is known as the spirit molecule due to its euphoric effects.

She was soon enmeshed in the culture. She felt hypnotized most of the time. They were using her energetically, but it wasn't until she experienced a full-on attack that she knew it was time to leave. She went home, and a distant family member called me to do a clearing with her, which we did. We disconnected her from the group's hive mind, released what she was ready to, and retrieved her lost parts. The clearing provided huge relief, but she needed to do further work. However, she did not return because she

*received a great deal of attention when she shared
her story and did not want to give that up. Her
family soon had her back on drugs.*

Some people have awakened but need information and tools to proceed into their mastery. Because
they don't know where to look, they can fall prey to
smooth-talking individuals. Sonya understood this,
and when she is ready, she will come into the realization of her mastery.

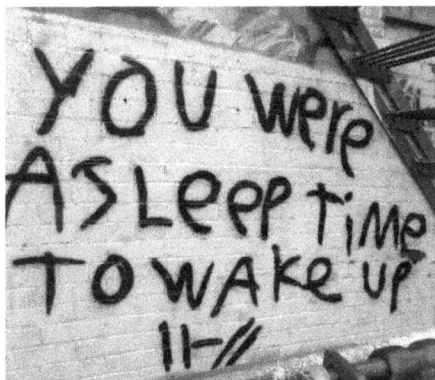

Art Alley Rapid City, SD

This planet, and everything and everyone on it, is
going through massive changes. This includes our past
life aspects; as we clear our baggage, they also clear
theirs. Things are righting themselves, and when we
emerge from this transition, we will see the benefits,

but for now, it leaves us questioning how we fit in when our reality is being shaken to its core.

Perhaps we have been asking the wrong question. "What if it isn't about what's 'out there,' but what's 'inside' that matters?"

The Why

You are awake. That was a bold move, but what comes next? Why take another step toward realization? What's the big deal anyway, especially when enlightenment does not guarantee a stress-free life?

If you struggle to find purpose, take a step back to gain a broader perspective. Start by focusing on something you are grateful for and immerse yourself in that feeling. Then, allow the deep inner joy accompanying it to permeate you for no reason, just because you can. From this space, the bigger picture will begin to reveal itself.

Embracing gratitude and joy expands our perspective, revealing a world of possibilities that inspire us to make changes. This mindset is far more fulfilling than looking back at the end of our lives, burdened by regrets for things we wish we had done. By acting now, we can create a rewarding life. Don't wait—seize the moment and eliminate future regrets.

We are often unaware of the broader picture when focused on our daily lives and experiences. But as we raise our frequency, we gain a broader perspective and illuminate greater potentials. While we do this for ourselves, we are also blazing the proverbial trail for those who follow. Without even trying, we affect everything around us and make the path easier for others. We are not trying to change anyone or anything; it simply happens as a result of living authentically.

Someone said, "Never doubt the value of the human body." That statement triggered a few thoughts. As we have discussed, we are in physical form to have various experiences that only this reality can provide. However, let's broaden our perspective and consider another value of our existence here.

No changes can be made in this physical world without an embodied being doing them. Disincarnate beings, angels, and ascended masters, regardless of their elevated status or past incarnations, do not possess the right or ability to alter anything in the physical reality. Only we, in bodily form, have that unique capability. However, a non-corporeal entity can influence humans to do what they wish for better or worse.

We often perceive ourselves as powerless individuals lacking any real authority, even though we possess it all. This mindset is just another layer of the illusion we have accepted. It's time to break free from this programming and recognize our sovereignty.

Challenges may arise after we recognize our mastery, but we can handle them with less effort, as there is no longer any need for drama, suffering, or struggle. Being surrounded by 'muggles' can be challenging, but it gets easier when we release responsibility for and judgment of them.

Many individuals strive tirelessly to perfect their human self, believing their efforts will be rewarded after death. Being the embodied master is not about perfecting the human because that is not possible. In this reality, there is always more to learn, heal, and achieve. Humans were never meant to be perfect, and what is 'perfect' anyway? Everyone has a different definition of what that means based on their background.

You will know when you finish your human incarnations because you will be at peace with your earthly lives. You will feel closure. You will be grateful for the broad range of experiences you have had, whether they were painful, insightful, burdensome, or extraordinary. All too often, it's only in hindsight that we recognize the value of our time on Earth.

Although we have always been realized, we haven't accepted it. Coming into our enlightenment is like writing a novel. We start with a premise. We know the ending, then we go back and create the timeline, fill in the details, give the characters life, and flesh out the story that leads to the conclusion.

As the author of our story, our master self always writes into the script everything we need to reach our goal. What we need always comes, but it may come in unexpected ways. "My Hut Is on Fire" is a parable from the Kamakura period (1185–1333) in Japan by Kamo no Chōmei.

> The *only survivor* of a shipwreck was washed up on a small, uninhabited island. He prayed feverishly for God to rescue him, and every day, he scanned the horizon for help, but none seemed forthcoming. Exhausted, he eventually managed to build a little hut out of driftwood to protect himself from the elements and to store his few possessions.
>
> One day, after scavenging for food, he arrived home to find his little hut in flames, with smoke rolling up to the sky. The worst had happened, and everything was lost. He was stunned with disbelief, grief, and anger. "God, how could you do this to me?" he cried. Early the next day, he was awakened by the sound of a ship approaching the island. It had come to rescue him.

"How did you know I was here?" asked the weary man of his rescuers. "We saw your smoke signal," they replied.

It's easy to get discouraged when things aren't going as expected, but we shouldn't lose heart because our energy is at work, even amid loss, pain, and suffering. That may be hard to remember when your little hut is burning to the ground. But it may be precisely what is needed.

You are awake. You know there is a better way, and you can no longer deny yourself of it. You have called for change, and it wants to come to you. Even if you don't know precisely what that is, you feel it right there on the edge of consciousness. You have prepared for a long time, and you are ready to be the master you are. That is why we take the next step after our awakening!

Mastery

Awakening is the beginning; it is the process of becoming aware of life's subtleties. After awakening, the next major step is embodied mastery, which is also referred to as mastery, enlightenment, realization, or self-realization.

The word 'master' can carry a negative connotation because some associate it with the context of master and slave. It is also used to describe a level of skill in a particular subject or activity. However, as humans, we can never master anything, for there is always more to learn, money to be made, healing to be achieved, and power to be had. Becoming a master gardener, a Reiki master, or earning a master's degree only indicates that a person has passed tests demonstrating specific abilities, not that they have achieved all there is to learn about the subject.

In our context, mastery is not about passing tests or controlling others, but achieving a deeper understanding and love for ourselves and others. Being the embodied master means bringing the light of consciousness into the physical body. Without it, our lives hold little meaning.

Mastery is not a goal to strive for; it is inherently ours, waiting to be acknowledged. The challenge lies in trusting ourselves enough to embrace it. This journey of self-discovery can feel like an exhilarating roller coaster ride, full of ups and downs. Therefore, we may choose to take our time and proceed slowly. However, realization can also unfold in a single defining moment.

Mastery involves seeing from a higher perspective and living authentically, regardless of external influences. We shed all feelings of guilt and shame, which allows us to love and accept ourselves unconditionally. There's no need to strive for perfection; instead, we relinquish the need to fix ourselves. With nothing left to improve, no goals to pursue, and no accomplishments to attain, we find ourselves contemplating, "What comes next? Keep reading.

Harmonious Collaboration

Our existence here is a harmonious collaboration of our human, our master, and our soul. The most familiar aspect of this trinity is the human body, which we can see and touch. It is the part of us that gathers experience. It engages with the physical world through its five senses and exists in a state of duality.

When we accept that we are more than just human, we become aware of our master selves. The master is the link between the human and the soul. It extracts wisdom from all of the experiences we have had. The master does not solve our problems, but it provides access to that wisdom, enabling us to tap into our unlimited potential. It exists outside time and space and is not subject to duality. Some refer to it as the light body.

The soul represents the third essential component of our being, embodying our inherent sovereignty. It is the very essence of our energy, manifesting in every aspect of our lives. Everything around us is a reflection of this energy, existing to serve and uplift us on our journey.

By recognizing that there has never been any separation between our physical body, our master, and our soul, we realize we are whole, harmonious beings of consciousness. This consciousness is pure awareness, transcending the limits of gravity, time, and space. This eternal is-ness only knows its existence as the ultimate and simple truth. Since it is not doing-ness, it cannot experience on its own; it depends on these facets for input.

Eons ago, we helped create this world of illusion. While this life appears real, it is built upon flawed concepts we have accepted as true. The greatest lie we have been living is that we are guilty, weak, and damaged. In truth, we are whole, complete beings. But just as scientists take things apart to understand how they work, we have designed this fragmented reality to explore the depths of consciousness and the nature of energy. We have gained the experience and wisdom we sought and are now ready to integrate our aspects. This results in our realization.

As a realized master, we love ourselves and know we matter. We accept all of our experiences without judgment. We know nothing is outside of us and that we have everything we need in every moment. We release anything that no longer serves us, including the need to process. We live in harmony with ourselves and all life.

The following statement may be of value as you transition into realized mastery. You can repeat it with focus and intention.

> *I open myself to receive my energy, which helps me fully step into my mastery. I have no fear. Nothing can harm me, and everything that happens brings me closer to full realization. I release my past to be transformed into wisdom.*

The pain, victim mentality, and struggles we cling to are not ours; they never were. They are part of the illusion. It's like becoming wrapped up in the characters' lives on soap operas, reality shows, or dramatic movies. Viewers feel as if the events are happening to them. This creates good drama; it is not theirs, yet they become a part of it.

If you have never been to a melodrama stage play, you can watch one on YouTube.com; recorded ones are not as fun, but you will get the idea. If you have, you know there must be a victim, a villain, a hero, and an audience judging the situation for the play to succeed.

The melodrama is an excellent example of life in this reality. We all play various roles at different times. We may be the perpetrator in one situation, the victim in another, and the hero in another. We also judge people and the drama around us. Just as in the melodrama, we get involved by yelling, booing, hissing, and, at times, sweetly saying, "Ahhhhh."

All characters are essential, but the audience makes or breaks the play. How people respond to the drama they see on stage breathes life into the performance. Life is like that. We spend a lot of time judging ourselves and others, never realizing that these are just roles everyone is playing.

As the grand fragmentation experiment comes to an end, we are ready to integrate all our aspects. We allow our realized master self, which was set aside for the experiment, to fully integrate with our human self. This provides us access to the wisdom we have gathered throughout our lifetimes.

Our Final Frontier

Gene Roddenberry created the television series *Star Trek*, and the Starship Enterprise was given the mission to explore new worlds and civilizations, going where no one had gone before.

> *Space, the final frontier. These are the voyages of the Starship Enterprise. Its continuing mission is to explore strange new worlds, seek out new life and new civilizations, and boldly go where no man has gone before.*
>
> Star Trek's Opening Theme

The journey through space provided the crew of the Enterprise with countless extraordinary adventures, yet our exploration of consciousness surpasses them as the ultimate quest.

We are on the brink of completing the integration of body, master, and soul. This transformative experience gives us the choice to continue our adventures in this physical reality as an embodied master or to ascend into other realms of existence.

Traversing your final frontier begins by saying, "I Matter."

Chapter 4
Open and Allow

One of the final hurdles to realization is allowing. In allowing, the person lets go of everything and simply allows I AM, divinity, into their life.

Adamus Saint-Germain/
Geoffrey Hoppe

Our lives become much easier when we open and allow. This may sound crazy when we consider all the scary things 'out there' that we might be letting into our lives. However, when we say we open and allow, what we are really opening to is our divinity because everything is our energy.

We are allowing our divine selves to bring everything we need to thrive in this world while becoming enlightened beings. This process of opening does not require us to learn new skills; instead, it invites us to rediscover what once came effortlessly. Embracing this truth can profoundly change how we navigate the world.

We have not been in our natural state for so long that allowing feels foreign and threatening. Instead of trusting our true selves, we have been opening to and trusting people and things. We have learned this was not safe. In this lifetime alone, we have let our guard down and gotten hurt many times. As this happened again and again, we developed ways to cope.

We might have remained open to the pain and suffered as victims. Alternatively, we might have retreated inward and become reclusive. Or we could have become bullies as a means of exerting control. To become conscious beings, we must trust ourselves and release our reliance on coping mechanisms.

We are learning that allowing does not mean letting others or circumstances dictate our lives. It's about being firmly grounded in ourselves, ensuring that those who seek to control, manipulate, or bully us will move on. It involves our soul, our master self, and our human side working together to shape our experiences. When these aspects guide our daily lives, we will be in the right place at the right time. The following is a fun example to illustrate this.

My friend and I were touring Rancho de los Golindrinas, a historic ranch on 500 acres outside Santa Fe. We toured the buildings, and as we walked to the back part of the property, it started raining. We took cover under a roof during the heaviest part of the storm, and when it let up, we returned to the main entrance. We stopped under a canvas canopy and sat on a bench. We were looking at the brochure and reading more about the museum when I said, "Let's go." My friend said, "Just another minute." I got up and stepped aside, and just as I did, the canvas broke, and water dumped down right where I had been sitting. If I had not moved, I would have been drenched.

This showed me that I know where to be when I pay attention. By trusting our subtle senses, we are always in the right place at the right time.

Sometimes, we find ourselves in situations that would typically be harmful. Should we open and allow them, too? The following story may provide some insight into options.

While driving in Wyoming, I saw dark yellow-gray clouds ahead and knew I would soon drive into a hailstorm. I had driven in hailstorms before and knew their power. I looked for a place to take cover, but I was on the prairie, and there was none. I told myself I was okay, no matter what happened. I released the fear, and after driving further, I noticed the clouds were behind

me. I should have driven right into the storm!
How did that happen? I gave thanks and drove
on.

In the past, I have driven in bad weather countless times, often trying to change the conditions with
my mind. While I succeeded a few times, I frequently
felt the full force of the storm. After experiencing
enough of these situations, I learned to stop trying to
control them. Instead of fearing the hail, wind, and tor-
rential rain, I focused on knowing that I was okay. I
knew there was a possibility that I could be injured in
the storm, and I was at peace with that. I knew deep
within me that all was perfect.

These experiences have also influenced other aspects of my life. I am confident that I will be okay regardless of what challenges arise. Worrying and ob-
sessing over them can block our energy and hinder our
ability to address them effectively. Things may not turn
out as we would like, but ultimately, the outcome is
precisely what we need.

Life can be scary, but everything will fall into
place when we let our energy attract what we need. As
we embrace our inner master, we are no longer at the
mercy of external factors, such as the weather, other
people, finances, health, or life circumstances.

I acknowledge that this can be hard to accept, and I, too, have had doubts about it. The following is a quote from my journal, written when I was working through the disbelief that everything is perfect.

> *The last few months have been stressful because my whole life is changing. I know I can't resolve any of it by worrying or being in fear. And I know it's not a matter of keeping my attention off it or thinking positively. No! It is more than that. It is knowing that everything is perfect, no matter what happens.*

Everything always works out, AND we may have some adventures along the way.

The Mind

Throughout our lives, the mind has become incredibly powerful. We assign it many tasks, but the primary responsibilities we have given it are to keep us safe and ensure our lives run smoothly. This becomes an issue when we have different ideas of what that means or when the mind relies on outdated, familiar patterns to function. It feels threatened when we ask it to venture beyond what it knows.

If we ask it to take a break so we can tap into our inner knowing, it stubbornly screams, "Take a break? Open up and allow? You've got to be kidding!" It cannot allow any activity outside of what it knows, as that could cause it to lose control and everything to descend into chaos. Little does it know that things are already in turmoil, and they would smooth out if it took a break and allowed consciousness to flow into our affairs.

The mind will never acknowledge that it doesn't have the answer. It will provide us with information that is often based on outdated experiences. Or, it will search its databanks for something it can piece together. If it finds nothing, it gets caught in a loop and continues to cycle until we become exhausted. This is called 'worry.'

We cannot be open when the mind is operating in overdrive and making decisions it is not equipped to handle. It sees things from a narrow viewpoint, leading to stress and choices that often do not serve us in today's world. It does its best, but it was not designed to handle all the tasks we ask of it.

Fighting the mind or trying to force it to be still is useless. You can't win! The mind must be distracted so you can move beyond it for the answers. There are numerous ways to accomplish this. For some people, engaging in an extreme form of exercise or a creative project may be a way to bypass the mind. Journal writing, cooking, listening to music, staring out the window, walking in nature, or soaking in the tub may also help. You can try different things to find what brings you into the space where you feel inspired.

When we still the mind and let our inner master inspire us, we see possibilities that are so simple we wonder why we never noticed them before. We see multiple sides of a question, event, or relationship issue. As we experience the benefits and gain confidence, the mind relaxes its hold and releases the notion that it will be obliterated if it is not in control.

If we possess both a strong mind and intuition, they may conflict with each other. It's not about focusing on one over the other, but about remaining open. This allows for peace and harmony; we will know what to do, and the resources will come together to manifest it into physical reality.

Sensing

As the mind relaxes, we open to gathering information through our subtle senses. Long ago, I heard people discussing seeing energy fields, ghosts, and vortices. This was confusing because I knew things, but I couldn't say I'd seen them. Then, one of my mentors told me that we see in many different ways. He said people talk about 'seeing' something, but may not actually be seeing it. Instead, they are 'sensing' it. After all, we do have other senses; vision is just one.

Once I heard that, I realized I was 'sensing.' I learned to convert those impressions into visual images. I couldn't tell you how I did that; it just happened as I immersed myself in the feeling. It was the same with hearing. Over time, I learned to use all of my senses.

Most of us have one physical sense that is stronger than the others. Observe which physical sense you rely on most; that is likely your strongest inner sense as well. You can begin there and expand into using the others.

For lifetimes, we have explored energy using our senses and emotions. But over time, they have become clouded by misconceptions, outdated programs, and limiting beliefs. Receiving information through these damaged receptors has resulted in skewed perceptions.

The senses and emotions can be powerful allies when they are healthy and balanced. However, they drag us through life's highs and lows when they're out of sync, turning us into slaves to their whims. How can we be aware of the subtle energies surrounding us if we are not in harmony within?

We have five human senses, but we also possess many more subtle ones. By clearing our emotions and allowing our light to shine, we can access the subtle senses, such as beauty, wonder, and honor. Using all of our senses expands our perception beyond the physical.

As we open, our perceptions change, and we see a broader view of life. We see the beauty in simple things. We no longer need chaos, struggle, and pain; those things fade like bad memories.

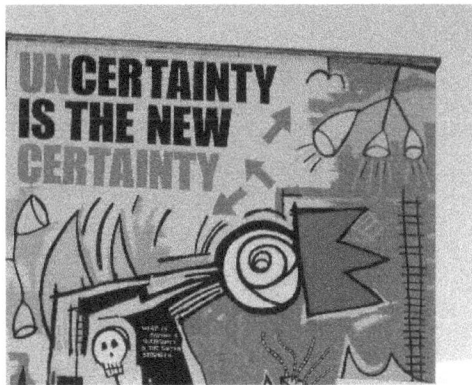

Larimer St Denver, CO

The Rules Change

The rules have changed. And they changed overnight! We used to be able to set goals and outline the steps to achieve them, then tick off each task as we completed it. It was a very logical approach to getting things done. And it worked. But now I can only say, "Good luck with that!" Is that working for anyone anymore? Perhaps a few, but if you like to plan and organize, and it no longer works, you know this is a major game-changer.

The rule for accomplishment today is that there are no rules. This represents a complete shift from how I was brought up, but I have seen how brilliantly it works. Being open and allowing the creative energy to flow has caused events to respond to my needs, sometimes without my even knowing what those needs were. Living this way is magical because we are always in the present moment.

In October of that year, I wanted to move to a milder climate. I looked online for rentals in Santa Fe. There was an ad on Santa Fe's Craigslist for an artist community in Arizona that was accepting applications. I applied and was accepted. In January, I put my belongings in storage and left my home, not knowing that it would be the beginning of a nine-month, 15,000-mile soul journey.

I arrived in Arizona and saw that the apartment they had available would not work for me. This meant I had no home. Now what? That was a question I raised many times during the following nine months. Before sleep, I often asked, "Which direction do I point my car in the morning?" The answer was always, "Rest, and the answers will come."

As I traveled, I met many helpful people on their journeys. Some came to my rescue as I set up my tent; one brought me fresh-squeezed orange juice on a hot afternoon, and many shared travel tips they had learned. After a stressful week, a person I had just met offered me dinner, wine, and casual conversation. It was perfect! People seemed to know what I needed when I needed it, and they were there to provide it.

I saw sites like the sunset in Organ Pipe Cactus National Park, Biosphere II, Tombstone, the ocean and wine country in spring, the new hospital in downtown San Francisco that we rushed to through construction zones at night in a rainstorm, and young artists from all over the country painting murals on plaza walls. I learned skills such as working with live-edge wood. The adventures came one after another; some were more fun than others.

Time passed, and sometimes money became a concern. At one such time, some friends were going to the casino, and I went with them. I wasn't sure why, as I only had $5, and I wasn't going to spend it on gambling! The lady at the service counter asked if I had a membership card, and as I searched my wallet, I found a $20 bill I had stuffed in a compartment months before and had forgotten. Wow! I had money to make the payment on my credit card! The casino gave me $10 in free play. I won another $30 from that money, so I had enough to pay my cell phone bill. This was not a large amount of money, but to me, at that moment, it was perfect and exactly what I needed.

I like having a plan, but there was no planning during that time. When I formed one, it always changed. I quit telling people what I was going to do because chances were I would never get it done. Instead, I said I was on a walkabout; some thought I was flaky. Perhaps I was! As I continued my walkabout, I began relaxing into living in the unknown.

Staying flexible and living in the moment allowed me to navigate various experiences and seize unexpected opportunities. During this journey, I was unknowingly shaping my new life, unaware of how each seemingly unrelated experience would ultimately weave together into a cohesive whole. After nine months of gestation, the perfect home in Santa Fe 'found' me, which was exactly where I wanted to be.

After experiencing numerous life transitions, I can attest that transition is not always easy; it requires us to remain open and change something, whether it is a habit, a belief, a home, a job, or a relationship. Some shifts we can make easily, while others we struggle with. Letting go of resistance and expectations will make the process smoother. When it is over and we look back, we can see the benefits and wisdom we gained.

I recently heard someone compare a person undergoing change to milk becoming yogurt or grapes transforming into wine. As we navigate any change, we may experience discomfort, but consider that delicious glass of fine wine you are becoming!

Throughout the process, we question letting go of hard work and struggle when we have bills to pay.

After all, the belief has been that working hard is the way to get money. If things aren't working, we must not be working hard enough. Many people think they have no choice, so they bring their shoulders up, lower their heads, and trudge through their day.

There may be days when you are shifting nicely; things are going well. Then, it feels like you lapse into old patterns of fear and worry. You aren't going backward; it's just another layer pushing its way to the surface so you can let it go. It is all part of the journey.

We could make the shift instantly, but most of us do it in increments. As we release old patterns, we rise higher in consciousness because it bumps us up another notch.

Imagine standing still and someone gently (or not so gently) pushes you. It moves you from that spot. In that brief moment, you feel off-balance, but you quickly regain your equilibrium and then move forward from that new place. Everyone has these moments, so don't get down and wonder why you can't stay in the uplifted feeling of flow; just keep taking the next step.

If you're going through hell, keep on mov-
ing, face that fire, walk right through it; you

might get out before the devil even knows you're
there.

If You're Going Through Hell
Rodney Atkins

This song often played in my head during my time on the road. I also heard it at gas stations and on the radio. It was my encouragement when I was walking—or should I say crawling—through some challenging situations. There was no figuring things out. The mind didn't have the answers, no matter how hard I tried to make it give them to me. I just had to keep going, even if I didn't see where or how.

I loved the adventure most of the time, but there were days when I couldn't say that was true. During those times, I rested, wrote in my journal, slept, listened to uplifting talks, and did what I could to maintain a positive mindset. One day, I was listening to Abraham's CD, *Getting into the Vortex,* and they mentioned our 'natural well-being.' That phrase struck a chord with me, so I contemplated and wrote about it in my journal.

I realized that I was beginning to feel better by taking my attention off the problem and focusing on my well-being. I continued writing. When I finished and went about my day, everything fell into place. The

issues I had been trying to resolve for weeks finally
came together. I knew exactly how to proceed, and
people were there to help. I wish I could say this lasted
the rest of the trip, but it didn't just happen; it was
something I had to nurture.

If the things you are learning and experiencing
seem difficult, keep going as best you can, and you will
be pleased with yourself when you come out the other
side. It is a very empowering experience.

Simplify

People who realize they matter often feel the need
to simplify their lives. They begin by discarding what
they no longer use. This has become so popular that
groups have formed to discuss a step-by-step approach
to decluttering their homes. They go through closets,
drawers, files, kitchen cabinets, under the bed, and the
basement; some even get as far as the garage and storage unit to discover what they no longer need. They
donate, sell, or gift those items. Re-homing things is a
win-win for everyone and a freeing experience. It is an
outer sign of the cleansing that is happening on the inside.

When chucking unwanted items, it is important
to consider the gifts people have given you. Although

these items may be beautiful, they can detract from the uplifting energy in your home if they carry negative associations. Similarly, dying plants do not contribute to a vibrant and healthy atmosphere. Surround yourself with items that enhance your environment and promote vitality.

An often overlooked area for decluttering is your online presence. If you have profiles on social media or dating sites that you no longer use, it's a good idea to delete the information in them. While you may be unable to delete the profile, you can delete any photos and personal data you've posted and deactivate your account. I'm not suggesting this due to some grand conspiracy (though there may be), but because these items require your energy to maintain them. Everything you own requires energy, just as a house requires the owner's attention, time, and money to maintain.

Some people are focusing on 'right-sizing' their physical bodies, which can feel overwhelming with all the other changes. Seeking the pleasure of comfort foods can be a perfectly human response in these moments. Listen closely to your needs, and give yourself the grace and kindness you deserve. Remember, this journey is not about perfection.

An increasing number of individuals are awakening to the importance of life's essentials and returning to basics. Even in urban settings, they find innovative ways to grow their food. Some are opting to become vegetarians. These changes may also be driven by rising food costs, causing people to make different choices about what they put on the table.

Many relationships are undergoing a much-needed transformation as individuals recognize their worth. It can be hard to watch certain people fade from your life, leading you to question your actions or even harbor resentment toward them. But resist that impulse. You are evolving into a version of yourself that no longer aligns with that relationship.

While it may feel isolating, remember that this is an essential period for nurturing and investing in yourself. Keeping that person in your life could drain your energy. Also, bear in mind that just because a relationship has shifted now, it doesn't mean it can't be rekindled in the future. Embrace this change as part of your journey to becoming your best self.

Many individuals are making lifestyle changes by selling their possessions and purchasing recreational vehicles to use as their homes. They don't want to be burdened by a mortgage and belongings.

The process of downsizing varies from person to person, but it ultimately centers on simplifying life and reclaiming personal freedom. By shedding the excess that drains our energy, we can focus on what truly matters, allowing us to pursue our passions and live a more fulfilling life.

Releasing the old can be exhilarating, and there can also be days when you feel anything but uplifted, especially when shedding emotional baggage. Don't worry, because that feeling is normal and won't last forever.

The following words are from my journal. Although I have moved on, I want to share them with you to let you know it's okay if you're not always upbeat. Also, I want to remind you that you can quickly step out of those moments. Here are a few items from the list that prompted my tirade.

Okay! Hold it! Back up the train! That is all well and good, but get real! My life is anything but sweetness and roses! Nothing can describe what I feel as I look at what is happening.

My photo editing programs all have issues, making it impossible to work on my art projects. The Windows upgrade failed to reinstall some programs and rendered others useless because they don't work with the updates. My Wi-Fi isn't functioning correctly, so I need to purchase a new modem, which I know nothing about. My phone is also having problems. This sounds like Mercury is retrograde, but it's not.

Thoughts that are anything but constructive are racing through my mind. I feel like I am drowning. I realize no one can pull me out; I must save myself! Even my inner voice is quiet.

I wallowed for a while, and then I breathed. I picked up my pen and wrote.

I had to climb out of the hole I'd tumbled into. As soon as I had one positive thought, my inner voice said, "Get real and get the book written. You don't have to have all the answers. Just share your journey."

I suspect these things happened so that I would return to writing. Since nothing else was working, I wrote.

I am grateful these times are rare. Being the master has its challenges, but it also provides the means to deal with them. It took breathing and thinking about the good things in my life. I felt gratitude for what was working and for the grace I had walking this path, even though I felt like a nine-month-old trying to walk and keep my balance. I wasn't always going in a straight line, but I was doing it, and I had to acknowledge that.

From this, I learned that no one can help us when we are enmeshed in fear or anger. It's not that they are punishing us; we just aren't open to receiving. As soon as we let go by having an uplifting thought, our energy is free to support us and show us the answers, and people come forward to help.

> *Think of the happiest things;*
> *they are the same as having wings.*
>
> Peter Pan
> J.M. Barrie

We have lived many lifetimes wallowing, so this is new, and any steps we take must be commended. So, give yourself a break and do your best in each moment, whatever that may be, knowing this does get easier.

At the end of your day, think of five things you're grateful for and record them in a gratitude journal. This way, you can use it to remind yourself that life holds many wondrous treasures. Snapchats of my great-granddaughters, a sunset, the sound of a gentle wind blowing through the treetops, reflecting on my stories, savoring foods, and dreaming are some of the things that help remind me of my joy.

Your list might include the things you have, your surroundings, the weather, or the challenges you faced; it doesn't matter what they are, as long as you have heartfelt gratitude. Reflect on each item and hold that appreciation for 20 seconds, allowing it to soak in. Taking the time to appreciate our lives uplifts our attitude and helps prevent depression.

Maintaining a gratitude journal can transform your perspective. On days when joy feels out of reach, reading your past entries can reignite your appreciation for life's blessings. It will help you feel better and inspire you to add more things to your list. Watch how it enriches your life.

Mindfulness Technique

How often, at the end of the day, can you easily recount the events of the last twelve hours, what you ate, what the sky looked like, what sounds you heard, or where you went and what you did?

If the day was outstanding, perhaps it was etched in your mind and heart, but all too often, it is just another day spent going through events with no awareness of or interest in what happened. I'm not saying this is necessarily bad, but by paying attention to the physical world, we train ourselves to be more observant of the subtle realms.

You can use the following technique to help you become more aware of your surroundings.

Perhaps you are going for a walk. The first thing to do is to leave your earbuds at home. Are you taking a coat, scarf, boots, or sandals? As you go out the door, do you lock it? If so, do you have the key?

As you walk, check with each of your senses. What do you hear? What do you see? Are there particular smells? Can you taste the air? How does the breeze feel on your face? What does the ground feel like under your feet? We take these things for granted and barely notice them. Your challenge on this walk is to be mindful of everything around you.

Another variation inspired by the movie *The Celestine Prophecy* is to pause at each corner and look in each direction, and see if one direction 'lights up' more than the others. Then go that way. You can repeat this at the next corner, keeping in mind the streets to get back home. I have done this exercise for years and have met some interesting people, as well as seen areas that I would not have otherwise. Incorporating this element into your walk can help develop your inner senses.

When your walk is over, find a comfortable place to sit. Close your eyes and bring to mind all you can remember. Did you talk with anyone? Did you stop to rest? How did you feel as you walked? Did anything unexpected happen?

A mindfulness walk can be a fun and easy way to develop your senses and expand your awareness. It can also help you focus on things other than the body's exertion, making the walk more enjoyable. Be mindful of your surroundings and remember to affirm, "I Matter."

Chapter 5
Ever-Changing Adventure

When you see someone putting on their Big Boots, you can be pretty sure that an adventure is going to happen.

Winnie the Pooh
A.A. Milne

Waking up often brings changes that can disrupt our lives and bodies, presenting challenges we didn't anticipate. However, you can rest assured that all is well, even when things look bleak.

Body functions, habits, dietary choices, and thought processes can all undergo significant transformations. Intolerance for manipulative, incompetent, and closed-minded individuals may emerge. Things that were once important may lose their significance. You might feel suffocated by your job, relationship, and living environment, prompting a deep desire for change.

During this transition, it is easy to become impatient with the conditions you are experiencing. Acting impulsively to force change can lead to feelings of failure and frustration, ultimately hindering progress. On the other hand, remaining inactive can breed a sense of restlessness. It requires patience to sit with these feelings, allowing things to unfold in their proper time while doing what is in front of us. By doing this, we position ourselves to act only when the timing and conditions align, significantly enhancing our chances of success.

Physical Signs

As light enters our bodies, it illuminates weak areas that need adjustments to hold that energy. Until they are ready, we may experience aches and pains. Often, these sensations come and go; we may eliminate one issue, and another pops up. These energies are not new—they have been lying dormant, and the light is pushing them up and out. The encouraging news is that they generally pass through swiftly. If they don't, it may be wise to consult your health practitioner. Or, it could be like Jamie's experience.

Jamie was having abdominal pain and went to the doctor. The tests concluded that she had a mass the size of an orange in her abdomen. The doctor did surgery to remove it, but there

was no mass, so he took out her gall bladder "as
long as he was in there."

Were the tests wrong? Did Jamie have the mass? Did it disappear before the surgery? It's challenging to explain, but this illustrates what can happen as the body prepares for the higher vibrations.

Another symptom may be never feeling rested. The body needs downtime to accommodate all it is experiencing physically and inwardly. Pushing the process will not help, so honor it and yourself.

Many individuals have noted changes in their appearance, experiencing facial wrinkles one day and a youthful appearance the next. Some find themselves fluctuating between weight gain and loss without any clear explanation. Vision changes prompt others to undergo eye examinations more frequently than before.

Some conditions that arise may be so intense that you feel you have been turned inside out. You look for ways to help, such as adjusting your diet, exercising, getting more sleep, consulting a doctor, taking supplements, or practicing meditation. It is good to consider these factors, but if they do not yield the desired results, it may be that your body needs more time to adjust.

A friend was experiencing lightheaded-ness; on one occasion, he even passed out. He went to the doctor, and after running twenty-two tests, they still could not determine the cause. Before they completed the weeks of testing, he stopped having the episodes. The lightheaded-ness left on its own.

The body must release low-vibration energies from past experiences to move forward. Think of the countless times you've fallen, skinned your knee, or bumped your head. Then, consider the times you were sick with the flu, chickenpox, or a cold, or faced disap-pointment and heartbreak. You were probably told to "suck it up" or "put on your big girl boots and get on with life," which you did because you didn't know what else to do. When we have these experiences and don't release the energy, it gets stored in the body and the energy field around it. At some point, we will have to address it.

Some people try to manage stress or pain with pharmaceuticals. If you need medicine, by all means, take it, and consider changing the circumstances that cause the condition so that the medication is no longer required.

Instead of waiting until all other options have been exhausted, we could listen to our bodies' needs from the start. It is our body—no one knows it better than we do, so trust its signals and give it the attention it deserves.

Some individuals are looking to their genetics for health answers. Much of who we are in this body results from our genetics. We are born of two people, each with a long lineage contributing to their DNA and, subsequently, ours. Our appearance, addictions, state of health, and blood type can often be traced back through our family lineage.

It is easy to understand that our biology comes through the DNA, but what about the characteristics we consider environmental? Where they came from may not be as straightforward as we think. For instance, a child raised from birth by just one parent displays characteristics and behaviors that belong to the parent the child has never met. Or consider the following.

At age two, Emily was adopted from an orphanage in another country and brought to the United States by a loving family. No one knew who her father was, but her biological mother lived on the streets and struggled with drug addiction. Quite expectedly, the child exhibited the physical characteristics of her mother, preferred the foods she would have eaten in her birth country, and displayed addictive behaviors. What was surprising was that at three years old, she began to show unexplained tendencies. One was the ability to work with unseen forces, and she used her gifts to manipulate others. Despite the therapies she received, the child was torn between her heritage and the values of her adopted family.

Many cultures revere their ancestry. They do not realize all that comes with holding on to the past and those who are a part of it. To free ourselves from this physical realm, we must release everything that binds us here, including our genetic inheritance. This does not mean we walk away from our family, but the genetic and karmic bonds that tie us to them must be dissolved.

This frees us from the karmic or loyalty bonds that tie us together and cause us to repeatedly incarnate into the same scenarios. We are no longer connected through guilt, obligation, neediness, or shared pain. We come together in mutual respect, recognizing that we are all unique, sovereign individuals. We develop a more genuine relationship with our family when we release these cords.

One thing nobody thought possible was that we could change our DNA, but Epigenetics has proven otherwise. We are not limited by the genetic codes we inherit at birth. By shifting our consciousness, we can redefine our reality. Further research will shed more light on this.

Problem-Solving Skills

Another change that may cause concern is that old problem-solving skills no longer work. Until now, we have relied on logic, emotions, and outdated programming to obtain answers. These methods may have been effective at one time, but no longer yield satisfactory results. We must go beyond them to achieve a higher viewpoint.

Often, a higher perspective emerges when we are relaxed. This inspiration can affect everyday situations, such as knowing when to pick up the phone and call someone or taking a jacket even when it's warm. It can also pave the way for transformative choices, such as changing jobs, relocating, or getting married. We all experience these inspirational nudges, yet many tend to overlook them. Since it is key to our new way of being, paying attention is in our best interest.

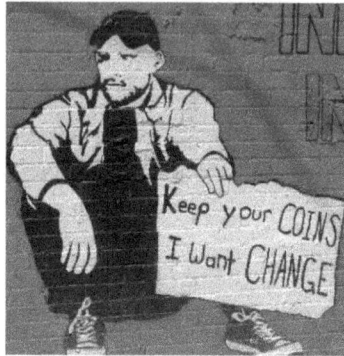

Art Alley Rapid City, SD

People can sense when change is imminent. They know something is about to happen; they may not know what, but they FEEL it. This awareness can be accompanied by a strong urge to take action, but what should they do? Trying to force action can backfire if the person lacks the necessary information or clings to outdated beliefs, fears, and guilt.

When we know things are changing but do not see the path forward, it is best not to push for a specific outcome. Instead, we can engage with what unfolds, creating space for clarity to surface. By releasing the need to chase solutions and attuning ourselves to the flow of energy, we can navigate this journey more easily. We are not forcing; we are allowing.

I had a major decision to make. Which path should I take? Both were equally appealing, but neither shone brighter than the other. I wanted both, but saw no way to have them without split-ting my energy. I became quiet, asked for a sign, made lists of the advantages and disadvantages of each, and discussed the possibilities with a couple of friends. Numerous times, I released the mental gymnastics I was experiencing, which worked until someone asked how that particular area of my life was going and threw me right back into trying to figure it out.

There was no figuring it out—the mind did not have the answer. I knew that, or I would have had it by now. Trying to find the solution only got me more confused. Eventually, I shelved the decision until after my trip to Santa Fe. I didn't need to know until then. Giving myself those few weeks' reprieve would take the pressure off and allow the answer to come.

During my time in Santa Fe, I connected with a friend. As we talked, I related one of my options to her and was surprised at the heaviness I felt. Something had changed! Then I told her

about my other idea. Joy filled me. It was so in-
tense that tears came. I had my answer!

The mind could not provide the solution. Perhaps
it wasn't the right time, I didn't have all the data, or I
needed the seemingly unrelated experiences that my
trip provided. By letting go of the need to find a solution, I allowed myself to absorb each of these experiences. I had struggled to get the answer, but when I
stopped forcing it and allowed things to unfold naturally, the clarity I was seeking came.

No one can say what is best for us. Well-inten-
tioned family, friends, psychics, and channelers all
have a limited view, especially if they are seeing things
through their own wounds, experiences, and agendas.
To see clearly, it is important to release our emotional
blocks and allow the highest action to be revealed.

I am not saying not to listen to others, because
they may be able to ask the right questions or say the
right things that help clarify the situation; however,
they can't provide our answer. That has to come from
us. Gathering input is valuable, but mindlessly following someone else's advice without evaluating its valid-
ity can lead to unintended consequences. Trust your
judgment.

If this resonates with you, take a moment to breathe deeply and immerse yourself in your inner quiet. Embrace the profound peace and calm. In this tranquil state, you will discover your truth. The answers are there and will come forward when you need them. Meanwhile, you can gather information, as a piece of the puzzle may be missing. Do all you know to do in a relaxed manner; answers will unfold at the perfect time.

Alone Time

As your intuition deepens, you may crave more time alone; honoring the need to retreat is essential for your well-being. Your encounters beyond conventional 'clock time' (the time we recognize in this reality) may become more frequent. This desire for solitude arises from your heightened sensitivities to the relentless noise, overwhelming energies, chaotic events, strong scents, and certain individuals. Prioritizing your alone time is not merely an option—it's necessary to maintain your inner balance and clarity.

People who are unaware attract chaos, victimhood, negativity, and strange energies, making it hard to be in their presence. However, as you stabilize within the new energy, you may find it easier to interact with muggles. Yet, you will no doubt seek companions who align with your newfound perspective.

As you withdraw from relationships that are not fulfilling, you want to be with 'your people.' You know and feel that there are people somewhere who know your heart and soul so well that you need never say a word; there is a connection, no matter the distance between you. There is great joy when you think about and feel their presence; you yearn to be with these beings.

Whether corporeal or unseen, trust that the bond you share will bring you together when the time is right. If you can feel it, know that the reunion is approaching. In the meantime, pursue what feeds your joy, knowing that everything unfolds perfectly.

At times, the emptiness can feel so intense that we don't always use discernment when choosing who enters our inner circle. When we allow those who disregard our worth and only seek what we possess, they can be detrimental to our well-being. Yet, driven by the need for companionship, we hope it will be otherwise.

Charlie's father died. That man was not only his father, but also his best friend, and Charlie could not get over his death. He craved the companionship he had with his father, and since he didn't have anyone else to provide that connection, he allowed people into his life whom he would never have otherwise. These people perceived his need as a weakness and exploited it to gain his trust. Charlie is a light in the world, and they sucked him dry, leaving him more empty than he was and looking for ways to fill that void. Drugs and alcohol seemed to work, which, of course, they sold to him.

One day, Charlie had a life-changing experience that caused him to quit drinking and drugging. After he stopped, he saw what it had been doing to his life. His relationship with his family improved, and his business grew, so he needed someone to help him. He chose a person who turned out to be a drug dealer, and soon, Charlie was back using and drinking. He knew what the outcome would be, but allowed his desire to work with another to overcome his better judgment. He then had to end that relationship and clean up the aftermath.

Charlie was a person who did not know he mattered. The realization of his true self was overshadowed by the belief that he was unworthy of anything good. How many of us resonate with Charlie's struggle? It's time for us to awaken to our true value and embrace the radiance within us.

As we grow in love and understanding of ourselves, we begin disconnecting from the collective consciousness and the burdens we have taken on from it. These encumbrances do not belong to us; we can let them go. Releasing mass consciousness is part of the transition towards integrating our human and master selves.

This may involve withdrawing from the hubbub of the outer world. It reflects our journey inward. While it may seem lonely, it is precisely what we need as we cultivate our independence. Once we have developed inner strength, we may choose to re-engage with the world.

Sharing Wisdom

As we gain a broader perspective, we see things others don't. Before sharing our insights, it is good to step back and consider whether the person really wants to hear what we have to say. They often just want to whine, take our energy, or gather ammunition for their next battle.

Your response might be to jump in with information and an offer of help. However, the most compassionate thing may be to step back and let them continue talking. By doing so, they might see the solution, because when someone has a problem, they also have the answer. They just might need space for it to surface. However, if this happens often, it could be time to establish boundaries.

If we share, we do it with compassion without attachment to the outcome. If we try to change the person, it will come back on us, so it's safest to remain neutral. Even when we see 'the writing on the wall,' remaining silent and withdrawing from the situation may be the most appropriate course of action.

Everyone's foundation of experience is unique. Since humans typically base their decisions on past experiences, their choices differ from ours. Even if they hear and agree with our perspective, they may revert to familiar patterns because they are unprepared to make changes. In these situations, avoid judgment, allowing the person to choose their course of action.

It is important to know when and with whom to share. If we provide the answer before a person is ready, they won't hear it. If they do listen to what we say, we set ourselves up as the all-knowing authority, leading them to depend on us every time they seek guidance. There is a wise saying that applies here:

> *Give a man a fish, and you feed him for a day; teach a man to fish, and you feed him for a lifetime.*
>
> Attributed to a Chinese Proverb

Instead of providing the answer, we can encourage them to connect with their intuition for their guidance. These individuals are on their path to awakening, and having been there ourselves, we understand the challenges that arise. And remember, as an embodied master, your presence alone can provide the energy they need to help themselves. Our role is to be present, allowing them to find their way.

To achieve an awakened state, we have felt it necessary to spend years doing self-work, and even then, it doesn't feel complete. As long as we inhabit physical bodies, there will always be more to address. The human will never reach perfection, and getting caught in the cycle of constant processing can be a trap. The obstacles that hinder our evolution will inevitably arise without us forcing them, so we needn't worry.

Scotland had been coming to my attention. Someone suggested I watch the "Outlander" series. I didn't know what it was, except that it had to do with time travel. I had put it off, but was looking for something, so I tried it. It was hard to watch, but I was hooked! As the drama unfolded, I felt the drizzling rain and the cold, damp air. I smelled the horses and the fires burning. I saw the green everywhere and heard the swords clanking as the men practiced. I felt the passion. Those days of rebellion had been my life. As I delved into the series, I dreamed of that time every night for a few weeks. Then it was over. I never finished the series.

We don't have to look for things to clear. If something is holding us back, it will come to light. And if we allow it, it will release with little effort on our part. It does not have to be complicated.

Throughout our journey, we have faced moments when we encountered challenges and did everything within our power to overcome them, yet we reached our limits and couldn't push further. Perhaps the timing was off, or we lacked the resilience and insights to fully resolve the situation. If this is the case, rest assured that the next level of the experience will come when you are ready to complete it.

Even if we forget the events, our body and master self do not; as they say, "You can run, but you can't hide." Our master self wants to squeeze every bit of wisdom from our experiences, which sometimes means a repeat performance. It will be in a new way, and we will have everything we need to make the most of the experience. We are wired to succeed!

Enlightenment requires us to release many attachments swiftly. Outdated theories, dependence on external validation, draining relationships, fear, uncertainty, confusion, and resistance cannot accompany us on our journey. If you feel stagnant or experience periods when your progress seems too rapid, take a deep breath, relax, and let go.

You are transforming, and there may be some growing pains. Be patient and ask your body and innate intelligence what, if anything, you can do to make it smoother. Then, pay attention to the nudges you get.

The cool part is that since you are already a master, you can't fail! However, you can do this with ease and grace or struggle and strife. When you're aware of what's happening, it's easier to relax and enjoy the ride! Don't forget to remind yourself, "I Matter."

Chapter 6
Energy Bandits

In reality, there are no enemies; we're all
souls in growth, waking up.

James Redfield

Energy bandits are forces that sap our vitality, undermine our motivation, and compromise our overall well-being. These drains manifest in numerous forms, each exerting its influence in unique and subtle ways.

It might be the driver in their flashy sports car who recklessly zooms ahead at the stoplight, the TSA agent at the airport who intimidates travelers, or that person who insists you'll never amount to anything worthwhile. It could be the friend who monopolizes conversations or only reaches out when they need to unload their burdens.

Sometimes, they are well-meaning folks with a backpack of experience. They may have good information, but sometimes speak from their past as if it will certainly be your experience.

My apartment did not have enough sun-
light, so when the lease ended, I chose not to

renew it. Instead, I rented a cabin by the lake, thinking it would be inspiring to take afternoon walks by the water. It would also be quiet for writing and provide a space with more light.

After moving into my wonderful sur-roundings, I had dinner with friends and shared my experience of the move, as well as how much I was enjoying my new place. The first response from an elderly lady was, "It will be cold this winter." Her second comment was, "You will have mice."

The temperature was often below zero, and I was neither cold nor did I have mice.

It felt like she was trying to rob me of my joy, but from her perspective, she probably just wanted to prepare me. If I had accepted her experiences, I undoubtedly would have had a cold house and mice. Then, other beliefs could have surfaced, such as, "Whenever I have joy, something or someone takes it; nothing ever works out."

Sometimes, a person's words and actions may appear harmless, but you will know an energy bandit by how you feel after the interaction. If you have been with someone and walked away feeling unsettled, you may be unable to identify exactly what happened; you just know that the encounter didn't feel good. If you feel drained, depressed, or angry, you have likely been bitten by a real-life energy vampire.

It is also possible that the person triggered one of your issues. Taking an objective look at the situation can determine if there is something to address within yourself.

When dealing with an energy thief, your first instinct might be to offer a deeper explanation in hopes they'll understand. However, be prepared: they will likely counter everything you say, making you feel even more defeated. Arguing is also a pitfall; you will never win because you are playing by their rules. You could remain quiet and let them carry on—something they will likely do. Another approach is to establish clear boundaries and communicate them confidently. If this strategy fails, without anger, walk away, thus preserving your energy.

Energy sappers are everywhere—in offices, social events, bars, street corners, and shopping malls. Recognizing their presence can help you conserve your energy.

A lady selling cosmetics at a kiosk in the mall called me over to her table. Not wanting to be rude, I went. I explained that I did not want

to experiment with new products; I was happy
with the ones I was using.

    She kept talking as if she hadn't heard me,
so I started walking away. She continued her
sales pitch and reached for my arm. Before touch-
ing me, she was being pushy, but she crossed the
line by grabbing my arm. I quickly excused my-
self and kept walking. It did not feel good.

If someone does not respect you or your space, it is up to you to take action to prevent the invasion. While it may feel uncomfortable to assert yourself, it is not your responsibility to accommodate these intruders. You have the right to set and enforce your boundaries.

You are the architect of your experience, and it is essential to acknowledge this truth in order to live as if you matter. You do not need anyone pushing their agenda on you; you are deserving and capable of taking responsibility for your life. Embracing this perspective will not only change your outlook—it will revolutionize your life.

We are magnificent beings, but we begin losing sight of that at conception, with our genetic coding and any past lives we may have carried forward. The next phase continues in the womb, where we absorb not just nutrients but also the thoughts and emotions of our mother and her environment. After we take our first breath, our experiences further shape and reinforce these initial impressions. By age twelve, these patterns, beliefs, and programs are well-established. They are reinforced as we attract people and situations that align with those beliefs. If we are unwilling or unable to entertain new ideas, we follow these programs for the rest of our lives.

While programming equips us with essential skills to get along in the world, it often fails to guide us in discovering our true selves. It makes our lives go smoother with less confrontation, yet to truly live free, we must acknowledge these cultural constructs for what they are—mere programming. Recognizing this allows us to break free and embrace our authenticity.

Changing one's programs can be approached in several ways. Some individuals choose extreme methods, such as drugs, surgical implants, hypnosis, or induced trauma, often seen in groups like cults and the military. These drastic measures aim for rapid change but come with significant risks.

In contrast, most people experience transformation through gentler, more gradual paths, such as counseling, meditation, or the arts. Although these

may take longer, they result in resilience and self-discovery, ultimately redefining one's life.

While there may have been valid reasons for
adopting the programming we currently have, we
must ask ourselves if it is beneficial in today's context.
It could be time for a shift. Until we do, we find our
lives dictated by the constant fear of the repercussions
for non-compliance, which is no way to live.

Drained on the Table

There is a group of individuals who can easily si-
phon energy while dumping their problems onto others. They are probably the most dishonest because they
should be more conscious of their actions. If they are
aware and do it anyway, they are disregarding the
other person's welfare.

This group includes massage therapists, energy
workers, psychotherapists, reflexologists, chiroprac-
tors, and practitioners of Reiki and kinesiology. When
we visit a bodyworker, we contract with that person to
focus on us and our well-being during that time.

With some practitioners, as soon as I got on the
table, they began imparting their political views, the
horrible state of the world, the disrespectful way someone had treated them, and other problems they were

having. At that point, I asked if we could discuss those subjects when I wasn't on the table. They usually understood and went on to provide a rejuvenating experience.

To benefit from bodywork, we must open our energy field. It is like a surgeon making an incision to operate. While we are open, we don't want the doctor introducing contaminants into our bodies. Similarly, when working with a practitioner, we are energetically exposed. We can be revitalized if the person focuses on providing a rejuvenating experience. However, if their problems consume their attention, that negative energy can seep into our field, leaving us feeling worse than before the session.

Bodyworkers should be aware of energy flow, but sometimes, they forget or develop bad habits. If they have no clue or continue dumping their issues and opinions after you ask them to change the subject, it is your responsibility to remind them why you are there. If they cannot focus on your needs, you may want to find another provider.

Power of Prayer

Many people say that witchcraft, spells, and incantations are the work of the devil, but is there a difference between these practices and the way some individuals use prayer? Prayer is undeniably a power-ful tool, but it is frequently used to impose one's will upon another. For instance, when someone appears to be making poor choices, their loved ones fervently pray for them to change their ways. Or when someone strays from their faith, the congregation intercedes for their return. These may sound like noble intentions, but we must ask ourselves if they are truly in the person's best interest. The requested outcome may not support their divine plan. (Later, we will discuss ways to help with-out intruding on one's sovereignty.)

Individuals who impose their will on others drain that person's energy, especially when their demands do not align with that person's needs. Since none of us knows another's soul plan, it is hard to say what is best. Regrettably, many of our prayers are often motivated by selfish desires. My friend experienced this firsthand.

Ann was staying with her friend in a small town in New Mexico. They had planned to visit the Acoma Pueblo, but another friend invited them to a party in Taos that same day. There would be interesting people at the gathering, and they both wanted to go, but this was the only day they could schedule a visit to the pueblo.

They called the friend to say they could not attend, and she suggested they stop by as it was not far out of their way. After much debate, they decided to attend the party and then go to Acoma.

They obtained directions from the email they had received (cell phones and GPS were unavailable at the time), but they had no idea how far "not far out of the way" was. Following the directions, they drove toward the house. They traveled farther and farther. The road turned from blacktop to gravel. It got narrow and bumpy. Road signs were nonexistent. A plow was working, almost forcing them off the road. Ann had lost her delight at going to the party when they left the paved road, and she was getting grumpier with each mile they drove.

She wanted to turn back and forget the whole thing, but she kept thinking they would be there soon, and this ordeal would end. The road continued far out of town. "How could this even be called Taos?" she wondered.

When they finally arrived at the party, a lady approached Ann and said she was so glad to meet her. The lady said that when she heard Ann might not be coming, she told God to get her

there and used all her power to will Ann to the
gathering.

Now, it made sense to Ann why she was
angry and didn't feel good about attending. She
was being pulled to the party against her will.
With this understanding, they left the gathering.
They reached the Acoma Pueblo just before clos-
ing.

Ann felt the force of prayer and the willpower
that accompanied it. When another wills a person to do
something, love is removed from the equation. The action is performed out of obligation and often in anger.

People who pray usually have good intentions,
but the problem arises when they think they know
what is best for another or believe they can be judge
and jury. In this life or another, it will come back to the
sender. This is called 'karma.'

Imprints

Energy sappers are not always people. They can
be imprints. An imprint is similar to a program in that
the ultimate goal is to manipulate and control.

Imprints are stored in the subtle bodies. They
don't magically go away when the physical body dies.

If they are not cleared, they are carried into the next incarnation. In that life, we may be angry, have unexplained pain or phobias, feel betrayed, have nightmares, and be defensive, suicidal, or apathetic. And we wonder why.

Considering that we have lived many lives, our imprints can be overwhelming. If you do not believe in reincarnation or simultaneous lives, think of this one alone and the many experiences that could have imprinted you. Imprints can cause us to get stuck.

The imprints that follow us from one lifetime to the next may be pleasant, but often they are not. They can cause us to be fearful, jealous, power-hungry, or resistant to taking our next step, as was the case with Thomas.

Thomas came to me because he was experiencing writer's block. We found that in another life, he was a monk whose job was to rewrite the Bible scriptures, removing references to reincarnation and information that would empower people. Guilt and shame replaced the message they originally conveyed.

He saw the damage this would do in the future and did not want to continue the work. He found ways to conceal the truth in the writings so his superiors would not recognize what he had done. Future readers who sought the truth could still find it, yet it satisfied his superiors. However, this was not enough to appease his conscience. The despair, grief, and depression got so heavy that he hung himself.

The church teaches that suicide condemns the person to hell. As a member of the church, Thomas knew where he was going, but that was nothing compared to the hell he was living. He died in depression, guilt, and hopelessness. These emotions locked into his field, and he tried to free himself of them in his lifetimes after that. In this life, he was still working to emerge from that hell. After we cleared these imprints, he became a well-known author.

Whenever we get into negative thinking, we subject parts of ourselves to hell. John Milton put it this way:

> *The mind is its own place and in itself*
> *can make a heaven of hell or a hell of heaven.*
>
> John Milton

If we have plunged ourselves into darkness, it can become a pattern for our future. We keep returning to lives that perpetuate that state to understand and integrate the wisdom and, most importantly, realize there is nothing to forgive. Once we do, we let it go and will not have to repeat it. The imprint dissipates because it no longer serves us.

Implants

Implants can be physical or etheric devices. They can resemble objects such as a crystal, fog, a computer chip, an energy ball, or a tiny device made of tissue and electronics. Some implants can result from experiments done in this or another life. We might even place them ourselves, as was the case with Martin.

> *Martin had a pain in his chest. When we examined the situation, we discovered a crucifix in his energy field. He had placed it there in another life. He felt he was a sinner and had to punish himself—he needed to suffer as Jesus had. Once he realized this was an old belief, he released the energetic cross, and his pain dissipated.*

Implants can easily be removed if we are ready to release them. Since we agreed to their implementation in some manner, that agreement must be taken into consideration. If implants are taken out before we are prepared to release them, we can experience confusion or a feeling of loss. When we no longer need the implant, it will slip out easily. There is no need to hurry the process or force an outcome. The body responds more easily and quickly when it feels safe.

These attached energies can influence how the person thinks and acts. He assumes the actions are his own, and since they are rarely beneficial, he judges himself as an awful person. Feelings of condemnation and self-doubt put him further under their control.

These attachments have two defenses. The first is that the person is unaware of their presence. They are safe as long as they can make him believe that he or another person is responsible for the chaos in his life. If they are discovered, their next tactic is to make the person believe they can do nothing about them.

We can change anything in our world that is not working. It may not feel like it, and we may not see how to do that, but we must accept that this is our life, and we are in charge. Once we open ourselves to that truth, the answers come.

We will see something we haven't seen before, someone will come into our lives who can help us, or the issue will resolve itself. When we say, "Enough!"

the situation stops because we don't need it and are not open to its influence. We are no longer victims; we become victors!

If the implant is a physical device in the body, surgical removal may be necessary. However, depending on the type of implant, it may be possible to deactivate it by raising one's consciousness to a level where it has no effect. There are various kinds, and they serve different purposes, making the approach and outcomes variable.

The Contract

Every day, we enter into agreements and sign contracts, seldom giving them a second thought. We make agreements to use a company's software. We pledge our allegiance to the flag. We arrange to meet friends at the theater. We sign contracts to buy a house, open a bank account, have surgery, get a cell phone, drive a vehicle, or purchase items on a credit card.

We enter into these contracts for many reasons. Some are necessary to get along in our culture; others are choices we make because they seem like good ideas. Additionally, we made agreements before we took on physical form—commitments we likely do not recall.

We entered this physical body with a list of things we wanted to achieve during this incarnation. To accomplish these, we made contracts with people who would play significant roles in our lives, such as our parents, spouses, children we would have, and authority figures. Whether we are conscious of them or not, all agreements were made because there was something we hoped would benefit us.

These contracts may have served us for a while, but we can let go of the ones we no longer need. An example of agreements that can become outdated is our wedding vows. What happens when the marriage ends and we remarry? If we have not rescinded the previous vows, they remain in effect. This can create a split in our energy with our new partner.

We have become so accustomed to contracts that we rarely read all the terms; many in the older generation can't even see the fine print. Some contracts contain hidden conditions, and we can agree to detrimental terms without realizing it. So, while most agreements help our lives run more smoothly, some are made with people, companies, or beings that bring us conflict and pain.

Not all physical contracts serve us, and neither do all inner ones. When we experience hurt, anger, fear, lack, depression, or shame, we want it to go away.

Desperate, we agree to things we would usually never consider. These agreements can turn our lives upside down, leaving us to wonder how we ended up in such a predicament.

To free ourselves from an agreement, it's not always necessary to remember it. As we become conscious, we automatically release the blockages that prevent us from realizing that we matter because they are no longer needed.

Self-Doubt

Self-doubt can hold us back in any area of our lives.

I had a concept for a book and was eager for feedback. I considered reaching out to a highly respected author, but I hesitated because her critiques were known to be quite harsh. Despite my reservations, something compelled me to share my idea with her. When she provided her feedback, her comments shook my confidence and left me doubting myself, my idea, and my approach to getting it into print.

I had been writing joyfully, and after this, I was stuck. I'd sit to write, and nothing came. I

felt I couldn't do anything right. The doubt was
so strong that I put the project away; it was some
time before I could open that file again. Why did
I approach her? I knew what she would say.

This became a significant obstacle to mov-
ing forward, and I had to find a way to get be-
yond it. I decided to write without worrying
about what I wrote or how it sounded; it could be
changed later. When it was ready, I would find
talented, supportive people who would provide
helpful comments.

I later realized that the harsh critique was
precisely what I needed, because I wasn't ready
to complete the project at that time.

Self-doubt can cause us to become bogged down,
yet it also allows us to identify areas that still require
attention. It prompts us to explore choices we might
never have considered otherwise.

Without self-doubt, we may think we have the
whole picture, but rarely is that the case; it is only our
point of view. Facts are relative and merely fragments
of truth. Remember the story of the blindfolded group
of people sitting around an elephant? Each touched the
elephant and described what they felt. They all had

different descriptions because they touched different parts, yet they were describing the same animal.

We condemn ourselves and others without realizing we are doing it. Sometimes, we believe we are stating the obvious, but the belief often stems from our outdated programs and old energy. NOTHING is obvious to everyone! If that were the case, we would all know that we are creators who have fragmented ourselves to live this grand adventure, and that everything has purpose. While this statement seems obvious to me, not everyone would agree.

We do not know why people do what they do. Most of the time, we don't even know why we do what we do! Why people are in their circumstances is not ours to judge; that is between them and their divinity. When it comes to us and our lives, it is a conversation we can have with our divine self without judgment. This understanding enables us to approach ourselves—and others—with compassion and openness.

Sometimes, we wonder why we even try; no one seems to understand or appreciate what we have to offer. We put our time and energy into things that seem to have no impact. Perhaps you cooked a great meal, and the family says nothing or doesn't even come to the table. You may have done a favor for someone, and there is no thank you, but an expectation that you do more. Sadness comes up, but you get on with life, wondering, "What's the use?"

We judge ourselves as having failed. But did we? Were our expectations of a specific outcome what caused us to feel that way? It may be years later when a comment is made that shows we did make an impact. The child, now an adult, may say, "Mom, I remember coming home and smelling bread baking or dinner cooking. You would give me a bite of whatever you were making. It always made me feel so good inside."

People may never say thank you, but if we are doing what is ours to do, it doesn't matter; we won't feel like martyrs. We take joy in knowing that we followed our passion and gave our best. If we feel taken advantage of, perhaps it's time to reevaluate our motives and expectations to identify what needs to change.

Sandy Seal Airbnb Florence, OR

The Shadow Self

We have the full spectrum of light within us. We are not just pastel yellows, blues, and greens, but also the dark purples, indigos, and midnight blues—colors that can appear to be black. To be whole, we need all of them; remember, white light is the combination of all the color rays. We may deny our dark side because we think we must be all light and love. If we believe this, we deny the strength our dark side offers. Only by accepting it can we access its gifts.

Sometimes, the shadow seems so dark that we want to run from it. We can never escape, so we may as well stop and confront it as Joe did.

Every Thursday, our group met to open a portal and bask in its energy. We took turns in this vortex, and as we did, information came through, healing occurred, and there was always some unplanned adventure.

One week, Joe was in the center of our circle and saw a dozen black things on the floor around his feet that looked like giant spiders. They were trying to crawl into his subtle bodies. He knew they were parts of him, but he was frightened to allow them to touch him, fearing they would take control and make him do evil things. He asked the group for support, knowing he had to let go of his judgment.

They were his aspects, and he was missing parts of himself as long as he kept them from returning. The group told him to let one touch him and see what happened; they were there to help if he needed it. Joe gave permission and let one touch his foot, and then his leg. As he did, the spider turned to light. Then he let another and another. As each touched him, it turned to pure light essence, not the polarized light, but pure white light, which he absorbed. A wave of joy flooded through him as he welcomed these parts he had cast aside.

After this experience, Joe knew beyond any doubt that we are divine beings and that nothing can harm or compel us to do anything against our will. To believe otherwise is to deny our sovereignty and live in victimhood.

Our shadow side has suffered as a result of our light aspect trying to coerce it into being something it is not. When we impose our will, we do not honor the role that part was designed to play. This misuse of force not only wounds but also deepens our fragmentation. This is when blackness comes in to fill the void.

If you feel darkness, check your body to see where it is stored. When you find it, intend that it gets whatever it needs. Don't force anything to happen. Just allow. Your innate intelligence knows exactly what to do, so let it guide you.

When we provide what the dark side needs, it integrates with our fragmented aspects. As they come into balance, there is wisdom and strength that surpasses that of the light side alone.

There is light and dark within us; no one is totally one or the other. Since we live in a world of duality, one can't exist without the other. To have light, we must also have the dark. We only access a part of ourselves if we refuse to accept both sides of us.

If you like visual images, the end of the movie *The Dark Crystal*, directed by Jim Henson, beautifully illustrates this integration. When we allow the polarized dark and light to come together, they combine to form pure white light. As they do, we know beyond any doubt, "I Matter."

Chapter 7
Which Reality Do You Choose?

All great truths begin as blasphemies.
George Bernard Shaw

It was winter 1996. My friend came to visit me in South Dakota. She stayed for a few days, and the day before she was scheduled to leave, we realized we needed to visit Devil's Tower, Wyoming, which was about 90 miles away. Devil's Tower, also known as Bear Lodge, is a striking geological formation considered sacred by the Northern Plains Indians and other indigenous peoples.

Snow was falling, and the weather forecast predicted 8-10 inches, but we decided to go regardless of the weather. When we drove onto Interstate 90, the snow was already piling up. We commented on it and quickly forgot about the weather as we became absorbed in discussing why we were making this pilgrimage and what we would do when we reached the formation.

The trip went quickly, and as we approached Sundance, Wyoming, I suggested we stop at the rest area, as there would be no facilities open at Devil's Tower. As I began slowing for the exit, I realized we hadn't been driving in snow, but now, all of a sudden, it was six inches deep and steadily falling. We had somehow shifted out of one reality into another. We commented on it, thought it was cool, and went on our way.

We did not fear the weather as we drove to Devil's Tower. Our focus was on the fun of having an adventure, and it pulled us out of the snowstorm experience.

From this, I realized that there are many levels of experience within the same event, and our energy determines the one that becomes ours. Is it pleasant, fearful, painful, joyous, fun, or monotonous? This is often not a conscious choice.

Many realities exist side-by-side, and it is as easy to switch between them as it is to step six inches to the right or left. The reality we entered was just as solid and real as the one we had been in, so much so that we didn't even realize it was a different one.

If you view life as a struggle, you get pulled into that reality. It is very real, and everyone around agrees, "Yup, life is tough for you." Removing your attention from the 'snowstorm' and directing it toward other possibilities will raise your frequency.

For a while, the scenery may look the same—for instance, you may still be working at McDonald's, but the energy will be different. If you stay in your uplifted space, it won't be long before you vibrate yourself out of it and into a situation that better suits you. It is our right to change our lives. If you wake up in the morning with a groan, lie there for a moment and look at the possibilities for your day.

Remember, there are infinite potentials, and you can say, "This is the reality I choose."

Simultaneous Realities

There may be days when the world feels unreal; you feel disconnected from your body, your life, and the people in it. It's like walking through a dream. Things even look different, and as you drive through your neighborhood, you wonder how those bushes got so tall or when that housing development went up. On those days, be mindful and center yourself before driving or operating equipment larger than your coffee maker.

When I first experienced this, I wondered if it was a sign of dementia. Dementia, slipping back and forth between realms, is not uncommon for people who are nearing the end of their physical lives. They are becoming acquainted with the subtle worlds, and sometimes they get stuck in the subtle realms while still in their physical bodies. My inner voice told me I had nothing to worry about, that I was not delusional, but was walking between worlds, and I would soon get accustomed to it. I did.

It was not something I consciously tried to do; my master self provided the necessary experiences. The new world consists of multiple realities, and I could see pieces of them—hundreds of these snapshot pieces extending before me, to the sides, and even behind me.

For many, this world seems cut and dried, but it's anything but! When we focus on a single possibility, our perception narrows our options, even though they still exist. We navigate that timeline, and each decision we make determines where it leads.

This is not just happening in our present life, but also in our past lives; they continue until we integrate those aspects. When all our fragments come together, we can access all their experiences and wisdom, as well as our present ones.

Polarity, time, and space have defined this life, but they will be different in our new world than they are in this one. The mind may not yet comprehend this, but these constructs are no longer experienced in the same way. From our new vantage point, reality transcends the familiar confines of time and space.

We are in the midst of a profound transformation; our humanness is being elevated on all levels, and our awareness is expanding beyond what was previously possible. While it's challenging to predict how long this process will take, we approach it with an open mind and allow it to unfold naturally. By opening ourselves to this change, we acknowledge that it is merely a step in unlocking our true potential and accepting embodied mastery.

I say 'accept' because we are already masters; we just haven't realized it. Every experience we have is part of our adventure and ultimately helps us remember who we are. It can be beautiful, infuriating, shocking, and profoundly inspiring—all at the same time.

Some journeys seem to get off track. I have had trips like that, especially when my GPS went wonky and took me down back roads into out-of-the-way places with broken pavement and no cars or street signs. On one of these side trips, I saw a ten-foot chicken. When I later told people about it, they laughed and thought I was joking. On another trip, I found my way back and took a photo. These times certainly add to the adventure!

10 Foot Chicken Somewhere in California

Living in a surreal world can greatly benefit writers, artists, game programmers, and other creatives as they move beyond the mundane to explore other possibilities.

As you navigate the shifting landscape of your reality, it's easy to question whether you completed an action here or in another realm. Consider the familiar scenario of misplacing your car keys. You come into your home and drop them on the hall table, yet they aren't there when you return. You scour the house, searching for them. Later, when you return to the table, they are right where you left them.

These are instances when other realities seep into ours. I've experienced occurrences that my logical mind struggled to make sense of, and some defied any rational explanation. Perhaps you've encountered strange events that left you questioning your sanity, or maybe you brushed them aside as just another one of those bizarre days. Yet, it's undeniable that some seemingly crazy things can happen.

I picked a quarter off the gravel and put it in my pocket. Later that night, a dime fell out of my jeans. I placed it on my nightstand, knowing it had been a quarter. So, how was it now a dime? In some other reality, I was fifteen cents richer than in this one. The next day, both a quarter and a dime were lying on my nightstand.

Another time, I was going camping and placed a small lamp in the car. I tucked the light bulb, wrapped in a towel, under the front seat to prevent it from breaking. However, after I set up camp and tried to find it, it wasn't there. It was too hot to walk to the store to get another, so I decided to wait until it cooled off. Later, when I returned to the car to get my purse, I found the light bulb on the back seat! It had not been there earlier.

You might think I've gone off the deep end, but I assure you, what I have shared is true. You can look for logical explanations—I did, but found none. I'm sharing these experiences not to provoke skepticism, but so you won't question your sanity if you ever find yourself in similar situations. Instead, you'll marvel at what just happened.

These experiences happen when we shift between different worlds. You can usually resolve them by returning to the reality where the event initially occurred, literally or in your mind. Once you visualize yourself back there, you'll find everything exactly as you remember; you'll be back on track.

Another example occurs when you enter the kitchen and forget why you are there. Interestingly, if you retrace your steps back to the original room where the thought first struck you, clarity returns, and you're likely to recall why you made the trip in the first place.

Imagination or Reality?

Imaginary means not real, according to Google. Considering that everyone has a different view of what's real, it could be argued that reality is no more real than imagination.

Imagination enables us to envision realms beyond our immediate perception—realities our human senses cannot detect. They exist beyond the limitations of our five senses, but that does not mean they are not real.

Despite being told to "get your head out of the clouds" or "it's just a figment of your imagination," imagination plays a key role in life. Using it to solve problems, develop innovative ideas, and integrate experiences can lead to remarkable insights and breakthroughs.

Using our imagination adds interest to our lives. Dreaming and exploring unseen worlds can be a lifesaver, especially for those trapped in a nightmare existence; it brings hope and possibility.

It is often said that if you can imagine something, it exists somewhere. This connection between imagination and reality suggests that every idea has the potential for groundbreaking advancements or solutions, regardless of how improbable it may seem. By fully embracing our imaginative capabilities, we not only ignite creativity but also empower ourselves to bring those visionary concepts to life.

When we were young, our imagination knew no bounds. We built majestic sandcastles, played cops and robbers, glimpsed dragons in the clouds, and brought our dolls to life with tea parties. In those moments, the line between our fantastical world and what was deemed the 'real' world vanished.

My neighbor told me her mother's story, which may seem absurd, but it demonstrates the power of a child's imagination.

> *When Calista's mother was a child, her family was very poor. She wanted a bicycle, but there was no money for one. The Sears Roebuck catalog came, and she found a picture of a bike in it. She cut it out and sat on it, imagining it was an actual bicycle. She spent many happy hours riding her 'bike.'*

To Calista's mom, her paper bike was as real as any other. When we are open, imagination becomes the center of creation, allowing its incredible power to transform our reality.

As kids, we instinctively chose the realities we wanted to inhabit; it happened naturally. So, what changed as we grew up? Could it be that societal conditioning stifled that magical ability within us?

A New Way

As awakened beings, we see the world in a new light. We see the half-truths, deceptions, and downright lies for what they are. When we were in hypnotic slumber, we couldn't see the truth and accepted what the media, corporations, doctors, churches, politicians, family, and friends told us. Waking up can be disorienting, as this new world can be starkly different from the reality we once held to be true.

As your thinking changes, people may disagree with you. If someone has an opposite view on life, know that those beliefs were formed by their experiences, just as yours were formed by what happened to you. Reflect on where you were a year ago; did you hold the same beliefs you do now? With each event, we grow and change.

We can choose our life experiences, and each offers diversity and potential. We can live on the streets in poverty. We can live in wealth. We can take advantage of or be of service to others. Everything we desire is available in this reality.

We may feel sad, angry, frustrated, or hopeless when we witness injustices. No experience is good or bad; everything that happens contributes to our wisdom and the Book of Life. Just think of the stories you will tell when you leave here! Consider the stories you share today! The ones that get the attention are those that affected you the most.

Telling stories can be fun, but if the situation you describe bothers you, you probably have something to clear. You will see the event without the charge when you release the emotions connected to it.

For a long time, I had a deep sadness for the Native Americans who, in the late 1800s and early 1900s, were herded onto reservations and forced to give up their way of life, religion, language, and their children, who were taken to boarding schools. They were compelled to follow the white man's rules, but their spirits never bought into that way of living. They saw no way out, and this led to hopelessness, depression, lack of self-worth, and alcoholism.

Many of these souls have returned, yet not all reside on reservations. Some have returned as white men and women living in the cities, striving to make their lives work. While some have adjusted, others continue to struggle with low self-esteem, hopelessness, depression, and the grip of alcoholism.

Ironically, many of the Natives living on South Dakota's Pine Ridge Reservation today are the reincarnated white men who established the reservations. They are experiencing the life they created for others, yet they aren't faring much better than their predecessors. Depression, hopelessness, lack of self-worth, and alcoholism are prevalent. Moreover, suicide has now been added to that list.

That time in history touched my heart deeply because, in the late 1800s and early 1900s, I was a Native American chief in that area. I was sent to Washington, D.C., numerous times to negotiate treaties that were never honored. I, and others, left our lives in deep depression at having failed our people; we trusted the white man, and he deceived us. While there was nothing that would have changed things, it FELT we SHOULD have done more.

Because of the burden I carried, I chose to be born into an abusive environment in this life. One of the reasons I chose that childhood was self-punishment for perceived failures to my people. I needed to forgive myself. Once I did and let it go, it became clear: there was never anything to forgive!

I gained an understanding I never could have gotten in a gentler environment. However, when I had received all I could from that situation, it was time to release the suffering and move on. The old ways were replaced with a kinder, gentler approach to life.

Good Friday Crosses at Chimayo Sanctuario, NM

When we look at life, we only see a thin slice of reality. There is always more happening beneath the surface. So, even if life seems to be going down the drain, don't judge; there is a deeper purpose at work. By setting aside judgment, we open ourselves to vast possibilities, allowing us to reshape events we wish to change.

Souls make agreements. We may look at another's life and say no one would choose that. But that is our arrogance speaking because we don't know their path. None of us is a victim; we are all creators. If we criticize what another has created, we are not honoring them or their reality. The person has chosen their path for a reason, which is not ours to judge. However, I quickly add that if you feel called to help, then by all means, do so without pity or judgment.

> *The world is too big and too stubborn in its ways for any combination of us to 'save' it. All we are called to do is to act kindly, responsibly, and attentively.*
>
> Scott Russell Sanders

Each person has a unique way of serving in life. Some offer their time by volunteering, writing articles, or participating in rallies. Any contribution is invaluable, but as a light being, there is another way to make a difference.

We can be the light we are. While this may seem simple on the surface, by shining our light, we illuminate the shadows where ignorance and deceit often thrive, bringing them to the forefront.

Another way our light works is that innovative solutions emerge, revealing possibilities that were previously obscured. When we embrace our inner light, we foster transparency and inspire collective transformation and growth in our society. Embracing our authentic selves allows us to 'be,' without the need to 'do' anything.

A friend and I wanted to tour a facility in South Dakota dedicated to providing homes for approximately 5,000 preppers. I had no intention of living there, but I wanted to experience what the community felt like. There were many red flags, but my friend and I tried to get an appointment despite the many hoops they wanted us to jump through. We stated that if it was in our best interest to go, it would work out—it didn't.

Shortly afterwards, articles were posted about the lawsuits involving the company; many of the red flags we had sensed were indeed real. The truth was coming to light as residents, ignoring their nondisclosure agreements, began speaking out.

This is an example of how our light can have a positive impact on situations. My friend and I were not judgmental about the facility; we were merely curious about what that way of life would be like. Outwardly, we did nothing to change the community, but our interest shed light on the situation and brought issues to the forefront. You could say it would have happened anyway, and the timing was just a coincidence, but was it? Maybe.

Societal issues I had never considered before have come to my attention. Now I see them and know there's nothing to do — I just need to be aware without emotion or judgment. I am simply a witness. The Double Slit experiment has demonstrated that we can influence energy just by observing without taking action. Therefore, we should never underestimate the impact of impartially observing a situation. (Research the Double Slit experiment to learn more.)

In the afternoon, I sometimes lie on the couch, watching the shadows from the trees dance on the wall while listening to soft music. I feel at peace. I feel blessed. There are no shoulds, just pure contentment. I'm not directing energy to anything—I'm allowing the joy I feel to flow. A great deal can be accomplished simply by being.

Choosing Your Reality

Every moment holds endless possibilities. By recognizing these potentials, we can choose which experiences we desire. Rather than forcing an outcome, think of it as playing with possibility. The magic resides in allowing it to unfold.

As I drove through the Arizona desert, I thought about how the possibilities on this Earth are endless, just as the number of cacti seemed never-ending. I saw each cactus as a potential that represented a different choice in life. How was a person to know which to choose? There were so many!

As if in answer to my question, my attention came to rest on a saguaro whose limbs majestically reached for the sky. Further down the road, a flowering red ocotillo caught my eye. Later, a prickly cholla lit up brighter than the others around it. There were thousands of cacti! What made one stand out from the others? I wasn't choosing one over the other; my attention just landed on that one. If I had been in a different frame of mind, another cactus would have caught my eye.

Life's decisions can be that simple; we allow our consciousness and our focus to bring what we need at the time. We don't have to play the mind game of sorting through the options; we simply open ourselves up and allow the right one to come to us. When it does, there is no doubt that THIS is the one.

The following story exemplifies how this played out in a real-life situation.

> *Mattie was in pain and went to the emergency room. They operated and removed a blockage from her abdomen. This began a year of testing. When she told me she knew she didn't have cancer, the tests concurred. When she went into fear about having it, her tests came back positive. At one point, they put her on chemotherapy, which the doctor told her to keep taking "just in case," despite her tests being negative. For a year, she was back and forth between having cancer and not having it. These times seemed to correspond to her focus and beliefs. As of today, it has been determined that she is cancer-free.*

All possibilities exist in each moment; we consciously or unconsciously choose which we will experience. This is true, and that is also true. They exist simultaneously; which do we want to experience?

It is as simple as stating what you want. Once you do, don't dwell on the outcome; know it is as you have spoken. On *Star Trek*, Captain Picard frequently said, "Make it so." That can become your motto, too. You are in charge and can say, "I Matter. Make it so."

Chapter 8
Designing Our Lives

You cannot be denied anything that is perfect, whole, complete, and right for you when you are your Self first.

Dr. Ihaleakala Hew Len

How much of our lives do we create, and how much is formed by chance, karma, destiny, or the influence of others? The extent to which these factors impact us can differ from person to person, depending on the depth of our indoctrination. When we clear our programming, we can shape our lives, free from the influence of others and our past.

Steps to Success

Many books have been written about designing our lives. *Think and Grow Rich* by Napoleon Hill has sold over 80 million copies. Another notable work is *The Secret* by Rhonda Byrne, which has sold over 30 million copies. These bestselling books assert that the key to achieving our desires is to vividly envision and truly feel as if our goals are already ours.

Many readers diligently cultivated a positive attitude and created lists and vision boards as they worked through the process, and they achieved remarkable success. However, for others, nothing changed. So, why didn't it work for everyone?

The effectiveness of these books varied due to several factors. Those who approached the concept with skepticism or half-hearted engagement missed out on potential benefits. The law of attraction suggests that one's thoughts can shape reality, but it also necessitates taking inspired action—those steps motivated by true inspiration. Those who took tangible steps toward their goals typically experienced greater success than those who relied solely on visualization.

The next point to consider is that many of our desires originate in the mind, which frequently lacks the insight to discern what is truly in our best interest. The mind is not the dominant factor guiding us into our embodied mastery, so if what we want is not aligned with our soul's purpose, the mind's guidance becomes secondary. Our desires must harmonize with our consciousness and align with our soul's path.

Because some practitioners saw this as a mental approach to manifestation, they attempted to force their desired outcome, only to discover that pushing energy to achieve their goals was ineffective.

Another significant obstacle was the deeply ingrained belief that we are unworthy of having our dreams come true. While we may experience some degree of success, beauty, and ease in life, it is only a fraction of what is possible when we align with our true state of being.

Many individuals who worked with the principles felt they had failed. They didn't fail; it simply wasn't their path. These books presented many great ideas that encouraged people to break free from conventional thinking. They were a step into a new story!

Master's Creation

I was introduced to another method for designing our lives in the 1980s when I lived in California; we used it to organize an in-person seminar.

The only premise we began with was that we wanted to create a worldwide event. Our group entered a meditative state, opening ourselves to any insights that emerged. We shared our visions, while someone took notes to ensure that nothing would be forgotten or overlooked during the preparations. There was never any disagreement because the vision did not originate from our minds. There was no judgment; everyone's contribution was valued. For instance, one person saw rainbows, which seemed metaphorical, but it was recorded. It turned out that the wallpaper in the hotel hallway where the seminar was held featured rainbows!

People were inspired as they envisioned themselves in various roles—working at the registration desk, ushering attendees, and giving talks, and they took on that responsibility. We saw who the speakers were and invited them. We even knew how many people would attend.

This three-day event had numerous elements that demanded our attention. We followed this process with unwavering commitment at every meeting, culminating in a truly extraordinary seminar. The attendees described it as the most successful conference they'd ever attended.

This technique can be used in our personal lives to create our highest path forward. We enter our creative space, move forward in time, visualize the end result, and then return to the present to walk through the steps that led us to that outcome. This is not a mental exercise, which can cause us to worry and try to control the outcome instead of allowing it to unfold naturally. Visualizing from the end requires no willpower but helps us access and trust our intuitive insights. We relax in the knowing that it is all taking us to our goal.

Doing so unlocks a more organic and effective path to success.

Conversations among some of my friends often center on the political climate in our country and the people "stupid enough" to believe the lies. I also have friends who support the administration. Both groups are good people, but they view the world through different lenses. Since it takes a lot of energy to engage in these discussions, I tend to avoid them. Instead, I have found it helpful to direct the dialogue toward what we want to see, rather than what we currently have. It provides hope and elevates the conversation because we all basically want the same things in life.

A good exercise is to list or describe in detail your ideal world. Keep doubts and negative thoughts out of the writing and focus only on what gives you joy. You are not forcing anything; you are designing from the inside out. Fixing the world may be beyond our scope, but imagining our ideal can inspire changes; our joy can help create the world we want to inhabit.

If you don't enjoy writing, you can imagine, draw, talk about, or bring your ideals to life through any creative means you know. The point is to enjoy them without trying to force anything to happen.

Until now, creation has been limited to repurposing what already exists in innovative ways; it has been limited by what we already understand. New possibilities and creations emerge as more individuals shine their light. Because we let energy flow in ways it hasn't previously been able to, creation expands beyond what the mind can perceive. This opens a pathway for the new to enter this reality.

Creation is the vibrant energy within us, while manifestation is the physical expression of that energy. Creation is not about trying to make anything happen, and it specifies no time or outcome. The process unfolds, often without conscious effort, allowing us to experience what appears to be a miracle.

By staying in a place of joy, we radiate it and attract more of what we need and want. We don't have to know precisely what that is or how it will happen. What comes will be perfect.

For this to succeed, we must let go of fear and worry, as things cannot work out when we are filled with unresolved emotions. As we release them, we see options that we couldn't before.

Many of us have been taught that we will achieve our goals by working hard. Hard work is good if that is what you want to do, but know that it does not necessarily guarantee success or happiness. We may as well be joyful and do what we are inspired to do; then, what we need will happen in ways we never considered. So, let's rejoice in the mystery and allow it to unfold!

The Inspired Life

Inspiration comes from many sources—a hug, a great meal, a good night's sleep, a dream, appreciation, loving relationships, a walk in nature, deep breathing, or quiet time. It can be something someone says or does, an energy that flows through us, or an insight that impassions us. Whether the blessings we experience come from within or the outside world, we can use them to trigger more uplifting thoughts and feelings.

Everything that comes our way is guiding us toward our realization; it cannot be otherwise. We have been preparing for this moment for lifetimes. Stay the course; you're on the verge of the most fulfilling experience you've ever had. Don't give up now, and don't be deceived by what you see around you. The truth is there inside—you can feel it.

If you have tried to do things and they didn't work, it may be because they stem from old energy. Attempting to navigate your path using the same approach you've always taken is unlikely to be effective. You are now in a new energy. By doing what you are inspired to do, instead of what you have to do, things flow more easily, and you won't have to work so hard. The journey is unlike anything you have ever experienced. Embrace it and ride the wave.

We create all the time, but usually not consciously. When our minds are clouded with worry, fear, competitiveness, unmet expectations, doubt, and a sense of obligation, it becomes incredibly difficult to tap into the inspiration needed to produce anything extraordinary.

We can cultivate positive thoughts and feelings, or those that foster negativity. If you find yourself experiencing chaos, desperation, obligation, and overwhelm, you are not living an inspired life. When such emotions arise, step back and take a deep breath. There is always a better way; ask for it. You can nurture inspiration by remembering the following:

- *Know that you can't get it wrong.*
- *Relax and flow with life.*
- *View yourself and your experiences with compassion.*
- *Trust that no matter what happens, you will be okay.*
- *Be at ease; your energy is working for you.*

Living an inspired life requires immersing ourselves in higher energies where anything is possible.

Some people describe this as living from the heart, while others might call it living in 'la-la land.' Still others refer to it as accessing the quantum field.

There are days when we engage in activities that make us feel good, and we are enthusiastic. However, when we repeat those same actions the next day, the results can vary significantly. It's about being in the present and pursuing what ignites our passion in each moment. Take cleaning the house, for instance—while it may seem mundane, on certain days, it can transform into a surprisingly rewarding experience. Embracing the present can lead us to a more vibrant and fulfilling life.

It is impossible to compare our lives to those of others. Two people can lead similar lives; one may describe theirs as idyllic, while the other complains about their circumstances. It is also essential to acknowledge that we all experience highs and lows. Some days, we feel invincible and ready to conquer the world, while on others, we grapple with self-doubt and question our worth. Understanding this can deepen our empathy and encourage resilience.

An inspired life varies significantly from person to person and evolves daily, even from one moment to the next. Yet, the undeniable truth is: staying in the flow, being open to the myriad possibilities, and welcoming them with open arms will bring the highest results. It's in this openness that we can find our inspired life.

Energy

There are many different ways to define energy. For some, it symbolizes the mechanism that keeps our homes warm in winter and cool in summer. Others perceive energy as the force generated through physical exercise. Additionally, some people view energy as a substance that flows from the universe, accessible to us if we learn how to tap into it. Our interpretation depends on our experiences and our understanding of them.

Energy is neutral; it neither judges nor discriminates. Instead, it mirrors and amplifies our vibrations, bringing into our lives more of whatever we project. When we live in joy and feel good about our lives, that energy reflects back to us, attracting more good. Conversely, if we dwell in depression and project that vibration, the energy responds by bringing more negativity.

We do not need to pursue energy; it is an inherent part of who we are. Since it responds to our consciousness, it may not align with our expectations in terms of timing or form. Our desires are frequently rooted in a survival mentality, but consciousness provides what is best for us overall. Understanding this allows us to cultivate a deeper relationship with energy and its abundant possibilities.

Since energy responds to consciousness, it knows exactly what we need. Once we accept this, we'll find that we never lack anything, as it brings what we need even before we think to ask for it. All that we need is available to us right now! To most people, this will seem like a miracle.

When I first became aware of my energy at work, I experienced events that I couldn't explain. It felt as though I must have received assistance from an external source, whether it was the Universe, an angel, or another being. As I delved deeper, I began to recognize the role of my energy in those perfectly synchronized moments.

We have always had energy, but haven't allowed it to express fully. We access enough to maintain life, but think what we could do if we allowed it to flow freely!

Peace Pilgrim was an American spiritual teacher, mystic, vegetarian, and peace activist. Starting on January 1, 1953, in Pasadena, California, she adopted the name 'Peace Pilgrim' and walked across the United

States for 28 years, speaking about peace. During that time, food, shelter, shoes, and all she needed miraculously came to her. She had this to say about energy.

What I walk on is not the energy of youth; it is a better energy. I walk on the endless energy of inner peace that never runs out!

Peace Pilgrim

We can connect with the divine presence within us to meet all our needs. This inner source is the origin of our true strength and abundance.

Until now, we have had minimal influence over our experiences because we have continually recycled the same old ideas, programs, and limitations. As a result, nothing new was able to reach us. It's like a hamster running on a wheel; it's good exercise, but it doesn't get us anywhere.

When we recycle life, our behaviors become predictable, making us vulnerable to being manipulated by anyone who understands this. This concept is not new; history is full of instances of control and manipulation of the masses, unfolding like a dramatic saga on the world stage.

As masters, we no longer fall for the lies and promises of politicians, social media influencers, salespeople, or clergy. We are free from the web of mass consciousness. Looking back at this web from the outside, we see that everything is perfect. We can appreciate that people have experiences that are right for them, and we no longer feel compelled to fix anyone or anything, including ourselves.

Looking at life from this fresh perspective, we uncover new potentials. As we manifest these possibilities, we begin to achieve feats others deem impossible. Over time, what were once extraordinary events become everyday occurrences, elevating the collective consciousness.

Experience with Energy

I had been exploring the concept of energy and how we shape our world by allowing it to flow, when I had a day when nothing went according to plan. Nothing serious, but little things—lots of little things! Here is an inventory of that day.

> *I went to my storage unit to get some items, but the temperature inside was over 100 degrees; it was too hot to look for them. I left without what I needed.*

I had books on consignment. When I stopped by the store to get paid, their computer did not show that they had made a sale. They did not have the books or any record of selling them, so I was not paid.

I went to the car wash. It had been out of service, so I was delighted to see the orange cones were gone. I got in line, but a truck in the wash area was not pulling forward. Finally, I got out of the car and asked what was happening, and a man said they were working on it and that it would be ready in ten minutes. So, I went and got groceries. When I came back, it was still not open.

When I bought groceries, I earned gas re-wards, but the computer at the pump did not show them.

I went to a friend's house to watch a movie with her, but she was not home.

It was late when I returned to the cabin where I was staying, and I was tired. I parked in the garage, got out of the car, and locked the gar-age door on my way out. Later, as I was search-ing for something to eat, I realized that the gro-ceries, along with the garage key, were in the locked garage. There was no way to get into it

without the key. It was late, and there was noth-
ing I could do until morning.

As I turned on the television and sat down
to unwind, a mouse ran across the floor. It was
time for a hot bath!

We have been taught to be assertive to get our needs met, which often results in forcefully confronting the person or situation. This approach can lead to a battle of wills, leaving both parties emotionally and physically drained. I am not suggesting that we should be submissive, but rather that we should choose how and where we invest our energy. There is a wise saying, "Pick your battles." Once you do, proceed with finesse.

If I had entered my storage unit, I would have been hot, sweaty, and exhausted. There was no arguing about the books; the computer was the ultimate authority. (The books did show up later.) The car wash was broken, and no amount of yelling would change that. I had locked the garage door, and I would handle it in the morning. In the worst-case scenario, I would have to call a locksmith to unlock it. This was a frustrating day, to put it mildly.

As energy beings, we shape our reality. So, how did this happen? This is not the day I had planned; I don't have days like this. I wondered if there was an overarching theme to the events or if each should be considered a separate occurrence. I realized it was not each experience that needed individual consideration, but rather the overall theme that held importance.

I had started my day in peace and joy, so that couldn't be the issue. Or could it? Upon deeper reflection, I realized that I had begun the day with a positive mindset, and if I hadn't, I might have succumbed to stress or anger. That positive foundation allowed me to navigate the day's challenges more easily.

Before getting out of bed each day, connect with your inner joy. This sets a positive tone and allows things to flow smoothly. That's not to say challenges won't arise, but they don't have to rule your day. As a result, you will experience less drama and chaos, allowing events to unfold in extraordinary ways.

Synchronicity

One fun activity we can incorporate into our daily lives is the practice of looking for synchronicities. These are extraordinary moments when events align perfectly, leading to meaningful outcomes that often defy explanation. These instances, which we might label as coincidences, strokes of luck, or even miracles, serve as powerful reminders of the profound and mysterious interconnections that shape our lives. These experiences can enrich our perspective and deepen our appreciation for the world around us.

Synchronicity was not something I thought much about until James Redfield published *The Celestine Prophecy* in the 1990s. As I delved into its message, I began to witness the profound insights he described unfolding in my life. While I didn't fully understand the mechanics, I began to notice how commonplace synchronicities were. I suppose they had been there all along, but I hadn't noticed them.

The following is a heart-wrenching tale that could have ended much worse if events had not synchronistically aligned at just the right moments.

Arturo was happily married to a woman with three children, and he fully embraced his role as a devoted father. Kelly would be starting college soon, and they had moved her mother to their home to help with the children.

Before school started, Arturo took the family to Oregon for a vacation. A week later, he treated his wife to a romantic getaway in Puerto Vallarta, Mexico. However, tragedy struck when, just before their return home, he drank excessively and fell from the balcony of their fourth-floor hotel room, resulting in a fatal accident.

In the wake of this tragic turn of events, things happened quickly. A hotel guest they had just met contacted the US Embassy, whose assistance proved invaluable. They guided Kelly through the maze of paperwork and the intimidating police interrogation, ensuring that she could leave the country on her previously scheduled flight. Auturo's body would follow after the autopsy.

Tragedies do happen, and no one wants to experience trauma like this. However, timing and many synchronicities helped them navigate this shocking event.

For instance, the family had a memorable time together before the accident. They had already moved Mom, so she was there to help. Earlier that day, they happened to meet the woman at the hotel who had the presence of mind to contact the US Embassy. The Embassy assisted with the paperwork and intervened with the police. The timing of all events was impeccable, ensuring that both the wife and the deceased could leave Mexico.

Synchronicities occur in fascinating ways. They often feel like miraculous events orchestrated by a cosmic computer meticulously scheduling our lives. Many attribute these occurrences to divine intervention, seeing them as signs of care or punishment from a higher power. However, understand that an external force does not impose synchronicities; they are manifestations of our energy.

In the movie *The Celestine Prophecy,* a pivotal scene occurs when John, the main character, faces a fork in the road and must decide which way to go. As he seeks clarity, an inner stillness washes over him, and one path lights up brighter than the other. Choosing that path, he unexpectedly finds himself captured by outlaws. Initially, he is consumed by doubt about his decision, but he soon realizes that this twist of fate has taken him precisely where he needed to go.

How often have we experienced this? We feel a strong sense of direction, yet things don't unfold as we planned. It's easy for our expectations to creep in and cause self-doubt. We can't judge because we rarely see the bigger picture while we're in the midst of the situation.

When we overcome challenging circumstances, to whom do we attribute that success? Do we credit ourselves for the choices that led us to our desired outcome, or do we hand the praise to destiny, luck, or God? If we praise external sources without acknowledging our role, we risk losing parts of ourselves; we fail to recognize the creator beings we are. Never forget: your role is vital, and you matter deeply. Don't hesitate to remind yourself by saying, "I Matter."

Chapter 9
Time Is An Illusion

The world existed for me because I could see it. It existed for me as a result of the transaction between my mind and the sources of sense stimuli.

Talons of Time
Paul Twitchell

In the reality from which we came, there is only wholeness within the self. Within that wholeness, we felt there was limited expression, so to enhance our experience, we created the world of time and space. Then, we projected ourselves into it.

In this physical world, everything exists in contrast to its opposite: good versus evil, love opposing fear, and the past standing in contrast to the future. This duality has enriched our understanding of ourselves and life in ways that wholeness could not. To experience duality fully, we became deeply entangled in it.

We have fixated on the pieces, mistakenly perceiving this limited view as the complete truth. We have gained all we can from this experience, and now it is time to reclaim our wholeness. This transition is challenging because we have become so entrenched in time and space that it is hard to envision anything beyond it.

We gather and integrate the lost pieces of self and reclaim the scattered fragments of our many lives. When we are open, this will naturally occur under the guidance of our inner master. As we integrate these fragments, our timelines converge, allowing us to see a broader perspective. In doing so, we rise above the influence of time and fragmentation. We are whole, sovereign beings, and we know it.

Time Distortions

Quantum physics is not my specialty, but I have had many experiences that only it can explain. These experiences suggest the possibility of time/space distortions, parallel realities, and even timelines bifurcating or splitting. Multiple realities coexist, and time is far more complex than a linear past, present, and future.

Countless possibilities exist simultaneously. We check the calendar and are astonished that a whole month has slipped away. We immerse ourselves in a project and are surprised when an entire day passes without our noticing. On a road trip, the journey can stretch on endlessly, or it can feel like we arrive at our destination within minutes of leaving home.

We usually don't remember what happens in other timelines. However, as we raise our frequency, the boundaries between them begin to blur, allowing us to recall fragments of the alternate realities we experience.

We view time as a simple measurement marked by the ticking of a clock. As events unfold, we rely on the clock to measure their passage. While this innovation has undoubtedly streamlined our lifestyles, it also confines us within its rigidity. Its convenience can come at a cost, as countless individuals lament the feeling of never having enough. Getting trapped in the relentless march of hours and minutes can be stifling, limiting our ability to engage with life as we would like.

Our experience of time varies dramatically depending on our surroundings. In quiet moments, time flows like a grand orchestra performing—each element plays its part, and together they create a beautiful symphony. This shifts entirely when we are on a bustling farm, under the tranquil canopy of a forest, in the vibrant chaos of a city, or when visiting another country. Even within the same space, the perception of time can ebb and flow, proving that it is anything but constant.

We may also find that the rhythm of some areas is more harmonious for us than others. Eventually, we get off the time track and live in the present moment of a timeless existence. This allows us to experience multiple realities simultaneously.

I was driving through Denver, and when I approached the freeway exit where my father had lived, I experienced us having lunch at Wendy's. That was Dad's favorite restaurant; we had been there many times when he was alive. While having that experience, I remained fully aware of my surroundings and my driving. This was not a memory; we were doing it! I had popped into that timeline while remaining fully conscious in my present one.

Although it may initially feel overwhelming and confusing, it becomes a familiar experience. You may uncover profound insights during these moments, so welcome them.

Time and space are not as rigid as they appear; they are, in fact, fluid and flexible. While it may be unsettling to consider the existence of multiple realities, this awareness can serve you well. For instance, if you are striving to learn a new skill or tackling a project, imagine connecting with a version of you who has mastered that technique. By accessing the abilities and wisdom of that accomplished self, you can effortlessly draw upon the key to success and integrate it into your current reality. Let this awareness work for you.

Art Alley Ajo, AZ

There are places on Earth where you can be transported beyond time and space just by being there. One such place is the Great Pyramid in Egypt. In that space, the conventional understanding of time does not apply. Although these towering structures are made of heavy stone, there is nothing solid about them, making mystical experiences quite common. This was one of mine.

I was in the Great Pyramid with a tour group. While in the subterranean chamber known as the Pit, I was transported into another reality where I could see and hear the people in our group, but they could not see or hear me. This was terrifying because I did not know what was happening. Later, I realized I had experienced different realities simultaneously. It changed my life![2]

We might have been born with the codes that allow us to transcend this timeline, or perhaps we are 'keyed' to receive them at pivotal moments in our lives. The timing and manner in which this occurs can vary greatly.

Many people have such a solid attachment to time that they don't allow themselves to step outside of it. Others experience time travel but do not recognize it; if they do, they often disregard it.

It is not always obvious when we slip out of this timeline into another because it feels just as solid as this one while we are in it. While things appear the same, they may be off just enough that we question them.

---

[2] The complete story is recounted in my book *Modern Shamans: Own Your Wisdom.*

However, since we can't explain what is happening, we often dismiss it as a product of our imagination.

I had an encounter with time distortion in the 1990s, when David was my mentor. He taught me to consciously sense energies in the land, communicate with interdimensional beings, and experience many other fun and wonderful things. I never knew what we would do when I picked him up for a day of adventure. Sometimes, the lesson began before I saw him.

I went to visit David and drove around the park multiple times, looking for his blue Air-Stream trailer. It is worth noting that there were only ten RVs in the lot. In exasperation, I said, "David, if you want to see me, manifest in this reality." His trailer appeared right in front of me! He had taken it and himself outside time, appearing invisible until I called him back. Or perhaps with that statement, I entered his time and space—I was never really sure.

Many adventures beyond this reality await the brave human. If you want to have fun, put on your 'big boots' and pay attention to the time slips in your life.

Big Boots

Grasping the intricacies of time and the nuances of reality can be challenging for the mind to comprehend, so I am using stories to help clarify these concepts. One particular experience from years ago had a profound impact on my perception of time and space.

I lived on a ranch in rural South Dakota. Once a week, I drove 100 miles on Highway 44 into Rapid City to pick up groceries and visit my clients and friends. On one such trip, I had been following a pickup and an SUV for miles. I wasn't in a hurry. I was listening to a Wayne Dyer talk and was fully engrossed in it. I approached an entrance onto the highway, where a van was getting ready to pull onto the road. He waited for the two vehicles ahead of me, and when I got to the intersection, he pulled out. I swerved, and he slammed on his brakes.

Why had he waited for the other two cars and pulled out when I reached the intersection? By the startled look on his face, it was simple; he had not seen me. We were in two different realities. Like my experience in the Great Pyramid, I was fully aware of my physical surroundings, but he was unaware of me.

Would that car have hit me if the driver had not noticed me and braked? Based on my previous experiences, I would say probably not. On several occasions, particularly on country roads, I have encountered oncoming cars encroaching into my lane, leaving me nowhere to go. As we approached each other, we passed right through one another as if we were ghosts in that moment.

I am not suggesting that you try this, because if you try to make it happen, it won't, and you could be in a serious accident. These time distortions occur only when we are in a space between worlds beyond our conscious control. What I am saying is to pay attention to the incredible occurrences that unfold around you.

You might be invisible more often than you realize. Imagine walking into an upscale clothing store where a salesperson typically greets you with offers of assistance. But on a timeless day, no one approaches you; you feel invisible. Is it possible that, in that moment, you are?

Despite the clock ticking away the hours for everyone, there is no single timeline. Each person follows their own rhythm, and yet our worlds come together, allowing us to interact with one another.

Imagine you are at a community event and are looking for someone you know. That person has an information table, and you walk around looking for it. You don't find it, but later, while aimlessly wandering, you bump into your friend. Your timelines crossed, and once they did, you connected.

What is remarkable about this phenomenon is that events align, leading us to our future. For instance, among the billions of people on Earth, we find the person we agreed to marry before we incarnated. We often label these phenomena as luck or coincidence.

However, when we accept our true essence as embodied masters, we unlock the potential for these extraordinary experiences to manifest consistently and effortlessly.

Time Bifurcation

Numerous times in history, timelines have bifurcated, which means they have split. They grow further apart as time passes, coming back together when we have achieved what we wanted from the dual experiences. There have been thousands of these bifurcations throughout history.

One example of a time split that affected the USA is when George W. Bush was elected president, while in another timeline, Al Gore became the president. Another split occurred where Germany won WWII, and the Nazis are now in power.

A time split occurs when multiple realities present themselves. It enables the parties involved to explore various aspects of an issue, deepening their understanding and experience. Once the insight is attained, the timelines converge once more. Those involved may or may not be aware that this happened. The following is Shawn's story.

I pulled into a gas station and got out of my pickup. As I did, I glanced at the car parked next to me and noticed it was the same color and model as one I had had 15 years before. The person who was in it looked a lot like me. The car was filled to the roof with items that looked like he had been traveling.

As I walked into the gas station, I had the feeling that man was an aspect of me that had bifurcated fifteen years earlier and was now coming back to join my present self. It was not déjà vu, but recognition.

I remember when it happened. It was 2009, and I had a decision to make. My landlord passed away on May 30, 2009, and I was given the opportunity to purchase his house. I tried for months to secure financing, but the house was in such poor condition that no one would give me a loan. I thought it might be time to move on. I didn't know where I would go, but it was not here. I would not stay in town if I could not have that house. At that point, a part of me packed up my car and left.

Then, a client who had become a friend said she would buy the house, and I could pay her back. On April 20, 2010, she wrote the check. Over the years, I have remodeled the house and still live in it.

When I saw that car with the man in it, the feeling that was an aspect of me was strong; I clearly remembered that period of going back and

forth about where I would live. I had bifurcated,
and an aspect stayed in town while another left.
It was now returning in such a way that I was
completely aware of it.

A bifurcated aspect is similar to our past life selves. They continue their experience in their timeline, and eventually, when we end our fragmentation, all aspects merge. This may be confusing, but remember that the past, present, and future all exist simultaneously.

When an individual, nation, or the world bifurcates and gains a new perspective, they benefit from that experience. They move forward until the next pivotal moment leads to another bifurcation. Multiple fragmentations can occur simultaneously, resulting in countless branches of reality. Once we achieve what we desire, the smaller branches naturally come together, as we no longer need them. We channel our energy back into the main branch; however, we are often not aware of this.

Trouble with Time

People often say they never have enough time to accomplish all their tasks, which is interesting considering that time is an illusion. If it is an illusion, how can there be a shortage of it? This is the paradoxical nature of time, which can be experienced as both rigid and flexible. Our perception plays a key role; it can feel as if it quickly slips away when we are deeply engaged in activities we enjoy. Or, it can feel like it lasts forever during tedious or overwhelming moments, illustrating how our mental state can impact our perception of time.

It is true that there is a linear progression of events, and we measure them with our clocks as they tick off hours, minutes, and seconds. We record those events as yesterday, today, or tomorrow, but that is a limited, linear interpretation of time.

As we come into our embodied mastership, our concept of time evolves. We begin to see time not as a rigid linear progression of events but as a fluid, dynamic force that can be experienced in multiple ways. This shift allows us to step outside its limitations while still fully engaged with our present physical reality. We recognize that each day presents an abundance of opportunities, and there is always just the right amount of time available for us to accomplish what truly matters.

For those still grappling with the pressure of the ticking clock, below are some reflections from a writing exercise I did in our memoir group. The prompt was,

"How can I simplify my life?" In exploring this question, I realized that the most effective way for many to simplify their lives was to examine their thoughts about and how they use time. If time confounds you, without judgment, here are three questions to ask yourself.

- o Is being busy distracting me from something I want to avoid doing or thinking about?
- o Has busy-ness become my identity or made me feel indispensable?
- o Does the cost of busy-ness outweigh the benefits?

If you have answered yes to any of these questions, you may want to examine your situation to gain more understanding. After doing this, if you are ready to release the need for being overly busy, here are some everyday suggestions to help you sort out the question of time.

- o Use a calendar to make a reasonable list of tasks for the day. Listing too many things can cause you to give up before you get started, blocking the feeling of accomplishment. The calendar is a crutch; it is not your ruler.

o Leave time open in your schedule for unexpected things that may arise; you will need that flexibility.

o Avoid telling people they can call you anytime with questions.

o Consider what you have to do, what you feel obligated to do, and what you want to do. Then choose wisely what you do.

o Handle a paper/text/call once. Don't pick it up, read it, and put it back down. Take care of it then and there.

o Finish one task before beginning another.

o Organize your space so you don't waste time hunting for things.

o If multiple people ask the same questions, create a standard response. Then send a group text or email to them.

o Evaluate whether it's time to let go of your job, volunteer work, projects, social obligations, or relationships with people who demand your time and attention. Is it time to delegate some responsibilities? Our needs change, and so do those of others.

o Remember, what you do is an expression of you, but it is not WHO you are.

When I shared the list with my writing group, some members incorporated one or two items into their lives; implementing all of them felt too overwhelming. Over time, a few have revisited the list to add more items to their routine. So don't feel you have to use all of them. Pick and choose what works for you.

You can use this list to simplify and create the life you desire. Remember, your worth is not determined by how much you accomplish. And whatever you choose, don't forget to have fun, because you matter.

Chapter 10
The Matrix

The matrix is a system. It's a colossal multi-dimensional system of custodianship and control which comes in many guises.

George Kavassilas

The revolutionary movie *The Matrix* aptly states, "The matrix is everywhere; it is all around...to blind you from the truth. The truth is that you are born into bondage, a prison that you cannot feel, touch, or taste. A prison for your mind."

A matrix provides the framework for this three-dimensional experience. It may be a constructed reality, but our experience within it is profoundly real. While we are immersed in this construct, it is challenging to have an original thought. To embrace our true selves, we must recognize the matrix for what it is. Understanding it will help us break free from its pervasive, mind-altering influence.

The film depicts what breaking free from the matrix could be like. Picture Neo, trapped in the life-sucking pod, as he pulls the cords from his body—cords that tether him to that fabricated reality. While we may not have literal cords plugged into us, we do have programming that is just as real and keeps us connected.

Removing the cords represented his awakening, but it was only the beginning. He saw the truth of the construct, yet he still had to learn how to navigate within it. Like Neo, we too are awakening, and our challenge is to find our way in a world filled with illusion, all while staying true to our newfound clarity.

Before awakening, the matrix dictated our reality. As we lived within it, we fell into routines that prevented us from seeing different perspectives. The more we dare to alter our daily habits, the more glitches we start to notice in the matrix. Even the slightest change can open up new opportunities, liberating us from the limits of the status quo.

Breaking free from the matrix equals freedom from illusion. We all have our release triggers, which differ from one person to another. How can we know what those triggers are from within the construct? Like any question we ask, the answer comes when we are ready and willing to accept it.

Remembering

We have spent lifetimes forgetting that life in the physical realm is a construct, and then we spent even more lifetimes trying to remember that it is. We became so entangled in this existence that we lost sight of the truth. This has caused us to feel helpless and to forget that we are creator beings. We are constantly creating, even if we do so unconsciously, which often leads to less-than-favorable outcomes.

When we helped design this reality, we considered that we might get lost and need reminders of who we are and where we came from. So, we incorporated elements to help us remember.

First, there are codes in us that activate when the conditions are right for us to awaken.

Since breaking free from the matrix begins with self-love, we incorporated into our humanness a concept centered on self-care. Hence, every decision we make is driven by the desire to meet our physical, emotional, or mental needs. This intentional design requires us to prioritize self-care and fosters a deep, nurturing relationship with ourselves.

Self-love is the key to freedom from the matrix. This notion does not revolve around righteousness, narcissism, or entitlement. True self-love enables us to accept ourselves unconditionally, stand in our authenticity, and demonstrate the truth of who we are. It involves honoring ourselves so deeply that the external world no longer dictates our lives or self-perception.

We know we matter and are worthy of living a divinely inspired life.

I was reminded of the importance of self-care after being involved in a car accident.

> *I was rear-ended in a car accident, and the damage was minimal, so my life went on as usual. Then, I had another rear-end collision that was worse. That one totaled my car and injured my body; I couldn't ignore the damage to either. I didn't get the message with the first accident, so I got to experience another. That time, I got it.*

The first incident caused only minor damage, allowing my life to continue as usual. However, the second one was a wake-up call I could not ignore. It forced me to confront reality and take my well-being seriously. Our master self ensures that we get the most from our experiences and even has us repeat them if necessary.

Each day presents situations that enhance our understanding and wisdom. Some experiences are gentle, while others are more challenging; the intensity is precisely what we need at that moment.

Loving ourselves lays the foundation for loving others, creating a ripple effect that benefits everyone and promotes well-being for all. The Bible says, "Love your neighbor as yourself." The problem is that many of us do not love ourselves. So, let's begin there.

While unaware of our mastery, we were unwittingly conditioned to see ourselves as inferior and insignificant. I even heard someone refer to humans as 'useless eaters.' Accepting the belief that we are unimportant has allowed this to become our reality. This program is a product of the matrix simulation designed to limit us. When we are free from the matrix, we are no longer subject to its programs.

Mass Consciousness and the Grid

There is a layer of energy that surrounds our planet. It is the collective of all the thoughts and emotions of every individual who has walked the Earth. Every experience and its accompanying emotions are stored in this energetic 'blanket,' and they don't magically go away. Consider what this means! Love, hate, betrayal, truth, greed, kindness, shame, and righteousness have been collecting since the Earth's beginning. What was once a grid is now becoming a dense, all-encompassing blanket.

This energy influences us and our lives until we become embodied masters. We believe our thoughts originate within us, never realizing that most, if not all, are fed to us by the collective. Everything is impacted by mass consciousness, including the planet and the sun.

It may be a stretch for the mind to consider that our actions, thoughts, and feelings influence the weather, earthquakes, solar flares, tsunamis, and volcanoes. But considering that we live in a biosphere where everything affects everything else, it's not hard to comprehend. Nothing is isolated!

The Earth is the biosphere we inhabit. Biosphere II, located in Oracle, Arizona, is a model of Earth conceived by scientists, inventors, and futurists. In this 3.14-acre, fully enclosed structure, diverse biomes mimic the ecosystems of oceans, reefs, savannahs, and forests, all designed to create a self-sustaining environment. Just as with Earth, everything in the facility is interdependent.

A group of people lived in the biosphere for two years without leaving the facility. They found that when one element faltered, the entire system, including the human inhabitants, got out of balance. Biosphere II powerfully demonstrated the interconnectedness that governs life on Earth, revealing that our existence here relies on harmony within the system.

Biosphere II Oracle, AZ

Another example of this interaction can be seen with the annual motorcycle rally in South Dakota.

During the first week of August, people from around the world gather in Sturgis, South Dakota, for the annual Motorcycle Rally. Sturgis is a small town of approximately 6,700 conservative people. For the ten days of the rally, the population swells to 500,000 in a slow year and 750,000 in a busy year. People drink, fight, attend concerts, traffic humans, ride through the hills, and generally have fun and do things they would never do in their hometown.

These actions generate troublesome energy that needs to be cleaned up. After the bikers and vendors leave, the locals are left with the energy and trash that were dumped in the area.

A few years ago, I noticed the weather was becoming increasingly unpredictable during the rally. It seemed that Earth was managing the chaos that accompanied it as it was happening. The temperature got unusually hot or cold, the wind blew, and thunderstorms brought baseball-sized hail. At the time of this writing, the weather forecast for this year's rally is thunderstorms for eight of the ten days.

In our naivety, humanity has unwittingly initiated a cascade of unintended consequences through war, political turmoil, religious extremism, alarming apocalyptic predictions, and slanted media narratives. These actions inflame emotions that affect not only us but also the planet. At some point, they will need to be addressed. If we do not take action, the Earth will cleanse itself.

As we were waking up, we absorbed energy from the grid and processed it as if it were our own. Our master selves have been transmuting these energies, as well as our own, into wisdom. Through this process, we elevated ourselves and contributed to the purification of Earth's grid. However, the weight of mass consciousness does not rest on our shoulders; we can release this burden. It is time to recognize that this is not our responsibility. No more!

I Am Done - Rock Layout Badlands, SD

Virtual Reality

Having adventures can be a way to bring meaning into our lives. Adventure is generally considered an exciting and unpredictable experience involving a degree of risk. What that entails differs depending on our ideas of what is unusual, thrilling, and hazardous, as well as our tolerance level. Perhaps exciting and hazardous mean bungee jumping, extreme sports, seeing a mouse, driving in a storm, or adding cream to one's coffee.

Adventures can be life-changing experiences, such as getting married, facing a health crisis, traveling into outer space, or moving to another country like Iran. Or they can be small, like trying a new hairstylist.

In fact, my move to Iran in the 1970s was less scary to me than some of the hairstylists I've encountered!

Adventures can provide a welcome break from boredom and make us feel alive. However, if we depend on them to find purpose, we may spend our lives chasing the next thrill, which can distract us from facing something we don't want to confront. Whatever adventure means to you, one thing it is for everyone is stepping outside their comfort zone; otherwise, it is called routine.

Living in the matrix may make more sense if we consider the technology known as 'virtual reality.' This is a vast subject, but basically it refers to creating and spending time in an alternate reality.

The person or group that imagines the reality is the game designer. Game developers bring the designer's visions to life, transforming them into playable products. Then, gamers enter these immersive worlds, adopt their avatars, and form relationships with both in-game characters and other players. They create entirely new lives within their game.

Gaming is much like life. When we enter this world, we face numerous challenges and setbacks before grasping its complexities. The many different experiences keep us engaged for lifetimes, allowing us to explore and grow without feeling bored. This real-world game has been ongoing for centuries, and we have lived and died so many times that we are becoming weary of it. It's no wonder that virtual gaming has surged in popularity; for countless individuals, it offers an escape and an exhilarating new chapter in their ongoing life drama.

As players become increasingly engrossed in the game, the line between the virtual and physical worlds begins to blur, making the digital environment feel as real and immersive as the physical one. It often requires stepping back, removing the headset, and observing from the outside to truly grasp that this experience is a carefully crafted illusion.

When I first saw *The Matrix*, I questioned how artificial intelligence could take control. Now, as I observe the profound impact of technology on our lives and its rapid advancement, it's clear that we stand on the brink of a similar reality. Will we go down that path? Some may choose that reality; after all, it is undeniably exciting. The deeper we go into the virtual world, the question becomes, "Is this the next step in human evolution, or is it a step backward?"

Disconnecting

To disconnect from the matrix, we must recognize that this is a constructed reality. Once we accept that, we can see the agreements we've made that shape our experiences and the programming that keeps us trapped. They must be released, but how can we do that when we don't even know what they are?

The most insidious and destructive belief we've internalized is that we are worthless lifeforms. Our acceptance of it did not happen overnight. It took time for it to become embedded in our psyche and for the essence of being human to manifest as actual physical limitations. As difficult as it has been, it was necessary; without it, we would not have been able to fully grasp the experience of limitation.

We have gained what we needed, and it is time to acknowledge that we are whole, magnificent beings having a human experience. However, just as children can be shaped by repeated messages, we have been conditioned to believe that we are unworthy and must rely on external forces—such as gods, angels, rulers, crystals, spells, money, power, artificial intelligence, and priestcraft—to navigate our lives. Nothing could be further from the truth!

We have everything we need within us to live happy and productive lives. Embracing this truth doesn't mean we have to abandon all support immediately. When we accept the truth of our divine nature and inherent worth, our programming becomes clear, and we can release what no longer serves us. Accept that, and the game is over.

Our soul never criticizes us for past actions or how long it takes us to remember our divinity. There is no judgment, only experience. This is true for us and every souled being.

After disconnecting from the matrix, adapting to the new reality can take time. Outdated patterns and ideas do not translate into our new reality, and trying to force them into it will only lead to frustration. It calls for us to embrace change and adapt accordingly.

Some individuals feel trapped between the matrix and their true selves. They are wrapped in confusion and despair, longing to go back to sleep in the matrix, which is not possible. This sense of being lost often stems from a disconnect with one's core essence, which is our compass for guidance and direction. Remember, you don't need to have all the answers; if you open up, your divine self will illuminate the path, guiding you toward clarity and purpose.

We can open our minds by reading, dreaming, and contemplating. Talking with friends who share similar experiences can also help us gain clarity and insight into our perceptions. By exchanging ideas, we remind one another who we are.

Many excellent movies also help us remember that life is not as solid as we have been led to believe. Some of my favorites are oldies but goodies, such as *The Celestine Prophecy, The Dark Crystal, Inception, The Matrix, and What the Bleep Do We Know?* These movies trigger memories of who we are and provide visuals that expand our awareness. They help us think beyond the confines of traditional beliefs.

While we cannot force ourselves to remember our divinity, it's evident that countless individuals around the world are becoming aware that they are divine beings. As they recognize that as their true nature, the light they radiate is transforming our planet in remarkable ways. This collective awareness is not just a shift—it's a profound movement that is reshaping our world.

There is more light than ever on the planet, but that does not mean all is peaceful and without issues. In fact, the opposite seems to be true. As more light comes in, things look worse as it illuminates the dark corners of our society, revealing what needs to be addressed. In time, things will get better.

No one said life after awakening would be easy or pain-free, and it is only natural to be tempted to hit the snooze button, but don't! This is an epic adventure; you don't want to miss a second. Just know that everything flows more easily when we acknowledge the process and have gratitude for every experience. No matter how uncomfortable it may be, everything brings us closer to realizing our divinity. Staying awake and grateful allows the energies to flow, which reduces stress.

Safety

As we come into our enlightenment, it is important to feel safe; however, in this topsy-turvy world, that is not always easy. Recognizing that everything that happens is for our highest good can be incredibly reassuring. Here is a simple technique you can use if you feel stressed or afraid.

Take some deep breaths. Feel into the core of your being. Recall or imagine a time when you were safe, loved, confident, complete, and in tune with life. Allow that feeling to permeate your body, even into the tiny cells. Bask in its glow for as long as you wish.

Love yourself and connect to your core every day. As you do, the bonds that hold you in the matrix will dissolve. You will no longer need to struggle to put food on the table, maintain your health, or get the recognition and love you desire. You will refuse to give away parts of yourself to jobs, consumerism, the medical establishment, family, or friends. You are sovereign and free.

You see the matrix for what it is. This revelation helps you remember that you are I AM, allowing you to confidently declare, "I Matter."

Chapter 11
I Exist

Enjoy your experience of Enlightenment. It will happen only once. Take a good, deep breath into the I Exist.

Adamus Saint-Germain
Geoffrey Hoppe

I AM, the master self, and the human are one. There is no separation. This is what it means to be whole. I am the I AM. I feel the joy of I EXIST, and I am that. That ecstasy flows from me with no agenda. I experience and express it freely. No matter the human experience, there is always joy, and I feel it.

Take a moment to absorb these statements; let their essence resonate deeply within you. Remember, each person will have their own unique experience.

I EXIST transcends the physical and defies the limits of time and space. Our perception of movement between this reality and I EXIST is an illusion, shaped solely by the focus of our attention.

The truth is that everything exists, and has always existed, simultaneously within us. We have lost this awareness because human nature tends to categorize everything in a linear way to appease the mind's need for organization.

We are in the physical realm, AND we dwell in the I EXIST at all times. Once we fully embrace this, we can access inspiration and answers that were previously out of reach. We no longer need to figure things out; we simply know. This newfound clarity enables us to navigate life with less stress and to experience a more serene and purposeful existence.

This is the lifetime when we end fragmentation and emerge as fully conscious, realized beings. There is no need to worry about how this transformation will unfold, as nothing can prevent it. Every experience we've gathered has led us to this extraordinary moment, making it not only possible but our destined reality.

This is an incredible time; however, we find ourselves in a situation similar to that of a military veteran retiring from a long and honorable career, who must redefine life beyond that identity. What do we do now? How do we navigate this new chapter and use our accomplishments to forge a meaningful path forward?

Can we relax and savor the fruits of our labor now that the mission is no longer our driving force? There might be a period of transition that is unsettling; however, as we release old vows, outdated programs, and burdens of guilt, we open ourselves to a new passion — a deep, unconditional love for ourselves and the opportunity to radiate our light. The choice of how we express this newfound freedom is entirely ours.

The Fundamental Truth

The online definition of 'exist' is to breathe, have life, survive, subsist, endure, and eke out a living. Only one statement referenced the existential aspect of man. It read, "Have an actual or real being," which is rather vague. Our vocabulary seems to have replaced our infinite potential with a narrow survival-driven mindset. As a result, countless individuals perceive existence as merely a struggle to survive. This narrative is not only misleading; it contradicts our authentic essence.

The fundamental truth is: I EXIST, I AM that I AM. In this profound statement, 'that' means anything we want it to, making it all-inclusive. I am worthy; I am light; I am an embodied master. We harness immense energy by expressing our desires through the I AM statement. Therefore, we must be mindful of what we declare after that transformative phrase, as it shapes our reality.

I AM is consciousness—eternal and unbounded, transcending any notion of beginning or end. As an embodiment of I AM consciousness, we, too, are time-less and boundless, reflecting an infinite existence that defies the constraints of physicality.

I AM is the foundation of all that is. Since it represents *is-ness* rather than *doingness*, it relies on humans for input. Our thoughts, emotions, actions, and senses serve as the means through which we gather experience. These faculties enable us to explore the richness of existence and convey the depth of our experience to I AM.

The eternal nature of I EXIST could evoke the sensation of drifting endlessly in the vastness of space—a notion that may seem both monotonous and terrifying. However, this perception is rooted in our limited beliefs about time and space.

When we immerse ourselves in the essence of I EXIST, we discover that we are not adrift in a void. There is no blackness or negativity. All fear, pain, guilt, stress, and even cluttered thoughts vanish along with time itself.

Once, I was asked what I feared most. Thoughts came to mind, but they all led back to the fear of ceasing to be. That massive program is a lie that has kept us tied to this reality. Annihilation is one of the five fundamental human fears. The others are mutilation, loss of autonomy, separation, and ego death. However, we eliminate these fears when we fully embrace the truth that I EXIST. We are infinite! How can we ever be annihilated?

We have the ability to access our mastery at any time. However, we may hesitate to do so, fearing it means we must permanently abandon our physical experience—something not everyone is ready to do. The death of the physical body does not equate to achieving a genuine state of release. Death frees us from our present physical body but does not sever our connection to the physical realm.

We are finished with the physical when we realize we are enlightened and always have been. We can continue playing if we choose to, but we will live as embodied masters, free to enter and leave at will.

The Role of Joy

One of the tools we have to guide us in making decisions is joy. Joy originates from within and is an innate part of our being. It is not dependent on anything or anyone. No one gives us joy, though they may help us remember it when we have forgotten.

I had a phone call that made my heart sing. Looking at this, I heard my inner voice say, "It's about joy. Just keep heading toward joy. You will know the way because your heart will sing as it did today. Your heart felt full. That is what you focus on—not the event itself. You can always experience joy despite outside stimuli. Be joy for no reason other than I EXIST."

While people and circumstances may serve as catalysts, helping us tap into it, true fulfillment comes from within. We appreciate their support, but we should not depend on others to lift our spirits whenever we face challenges. Our inner strength and happiness are ours to cultivate and cherish.

When you feel joy, take a moment to feel it fully. Appreciate that sense of fulfillment, and let it flow through you in ways that resonate with your spirit. Whether you're tending to your garden, redecorating your living space, diving into an exciting video game, catching up with friends over coffee, or simply sharing a smile with those around you, allow that joy to illuminate your life. Celebrate it and let it inspire you.

We often take for granted the gestures of kindness others extend to us. Think about the messages of goodwill you receive through texts, social media, or greeting cards—how do you respond to them? Do you find yourself tallying the number of comments on your birthday post, feeling disappointed if someone forgets to send their wishes? Or do you skim through these messages, dismissing them without a second thought?

Allow gratitude to fill your heart and resonate within you for a moment. It may not always be obvious, but people do care, or at least they want to. They get caught up in their lives, but they mean well. Even when individuals extend wishes out of social obligation, they are taking the time, so do appreciate it.

Love and gratitude nurture and uplift our spirits, while worry and feelings of unworthiness stifle them. By focusing on our blessings and the kindness we receive, we cultivate a sense of well-being that enriches not only our lives but the lives of those around us.

Accessing joy amidst the worries and struggles we encounter can be challenging. When we do experience joy, society frequently pressures us to tone it down and adopt a more serious demeanor. This pressure causes us to fear having our joy stomped on or snatched away, making it difficult to express it freely. While it is true that misery often loves company, we must not let others dictate our state of being. Instead, we celebrate our joy boldly and unapologetically, allowing it to illuminate our path forward.

Living in this physical world can be difficult, but experiencing joy makes life worthwhile. As we live and express that magic into the world, it touches others and generates more.

> *Last summer, my patio came alive with bright, flowering plants. It was a delight to shop for and plant the sprouts, and I enjoyed tending them and watching them grow. They also brought happiness to those who walked by. People stopped to admire them, and I became known as the 'flower lady' in our community.*

This is an example of how we can do what we love, be of service, and shine our light all at the same time. Too often, service has been equated with suffering, but it doesn't have to be drudgery. It works best when it's a win/win for everyone. That is when all parties benefit.

Not everyone wants to feel joy. There are benefits to wallowing in misery; oftentimes, one receives attention and sympathy from telling sad stories.

A friend had not returned my calls, and I wondered what was up. When he did call, it was one piece of bad news after another. He asked me to cheer him up, so I told him a funny story. Suddenly, he had to go. He didn't really want to be happy; he wanted to complain, hoping I would join him in his misfortune. When I didn't, he lost interest in continuing our conversation. It was then that I realized most of our calls centered around his bad news.

I contemplated why he only wanted to talk about his troubles and realized that he receives a lot of attention and financial support by experiencing trauma and drama, and then telling the story. He is a lovable guy, and people want to help him, often to their financial detriment.

One day, I reflected on my life and asked myself whether I enjoyed it. I did; I could always tap into joy. However, when I considered my overall happiness, I acknowledged that I wasn't always happy. Then I thought about fun and recognized that there were indeed fun moments. We often think of joy, happiness, and fun as the same thing, but they have distinct differences.

Joy is a profound inner sense that cannot be taken away, regardless of our mood or external circumstances. In contrast, happiness is a transient emotion that can fluctuate in response to our experiences. For instance, a compliment might bring a sense of happiness, but those feelings can swiftly turn to sadness, anger, or fear upon receiving distressing news. Fun, meanwhile, is a momentary experience—an event that brings excitement but is often short-lived. Our activities shape our perception of fun and have the power to influence our emotional state.

Understanding these differences can keep us from setting unrealistic expectations.

The Attraction

Many beings yearn to incarnate on Earth, eager to experience the profound layers of humanness—elements we often take for granted or occasionally resent. Our immersion in this human existence has obscured the true significance of these experiences, yet within us lies a recognition of their value, even if it has been overshadowed by forgetfulness. If we remembered, we would undoubtedly live every moment with passion and gratitude.

It was not really Saturday night, at least it may have been, for they had long lost count of the days, but always, if they wanted to do anything special, they said this was Saturday night, and then they did it.

Peter Pan
J.M. Barrie

There are many reasons why beings want to incarnate in a physical body. For some, the motive lies in harnessing and manipulating human energy to further their agendas. Others are drawn by a desire to experience the full range of emotions and senses. They witness our happiness, sadness, pleasure, and pain, and yearn to know them firsthand. However, they underestimate how seductive they can become.

We created scenarios to experience a wide range of emotions, from the heights of pleasure to the depths of despair. We wanted it all, but unwittingly became trapped by these emotions. The good news is that we can end this cycle at any time by awakening to our true nature as embodied masters. Even after waking up, many will continue the experience because they find something of value in it.

Take a moment to consider what would be fun for you. As you review your list, note how many items involve the emotions and senses. I suspect that most, if not all, will be tied to them because they make human life unique.

Our experiences have guided us to total acceptance and profound love for ourselves. This love has transformed us. We stand as examples for others who seek this energy for themselves. At this moment, Earth is a prime environment for experiencing love.

Every night can be Saturday night. Claim it and remind yourself, "I Matter."

Chapter 12
Beginning or Ending

But that's not the end of the story. The best is yet to come.

Robert Fulghum

We have come full circle. We began this book by saying, "I Matter." When we say that, we are also saying I AM that I AM, I EXIST.

I AM that I AM speaks to the essence of existence and self-realization. This declaration invites us to recognize our true nature. It encourages us to shed labels and limitations that define us. I AM that I AM is more than an affirmation; it is a statement of truth that inspires recognition and self-acceptance.

I EXIST encapsulates the essence of self-awareness and consciousness. It invites us to connect deeply with our inner selves despite today's fast-paced and often superficial society. It encourages us to acknowledge and celebrate our existence by embracing consciousness.

Stay or Go?

As conscious masters, we can make choices we previously lacked the awareness to make. Once we realize our divinity, we can either continue living in this reality or leave our physical form permanently, as many revered masters have done. However, some have chosen to maintain a body to use when they wish to interact in this world. There isn't a guide for what to expect if we keep a physical body; the path is one of limitless possibilities.

If we choose to stay, we can decide how we interact with life. Do we continue playing the game? Probably not. We understand the game and have reached a point where there is nothing left to gain by continuing to participate. It marks the EndGame.

If we continue to reside in physical bodies, we will be living from a heightened state of awareness; our experience is profoundly transformed. Our bodies have adjusted to these higher vibrations and are no longer vulnerable to the pains and ailments that once plagued us. Working on ourselves becomes a thing of the past.

Beyond a mere mental concept, we recognize that energy supports us, and there is no need to force anything. We no longer push for outcomes, as we have learned that doing so disrupts the natural flow and creates unnecessary obstacles. Instead, we allow our energy to attract what we need. The mind becomes comfortable letting our master selves take the lead; through experience, it has learned to trust.

Some may choose to remain on Earth to leave a legacy for others. Their service will act as a guiding light and ease the journey for those who follow. Even if they do nothing, their light will elevate the planet's consciousness, laying a foundation for future generations.

As we reflect on our humanity, we realize we are entering a profound new era centered on truly loving ourselves. When we embrace this truth, we honor ourselves as sovereign beings, live authentically, and cultivate compassion for all. This expanded understanding of love transforms not only our relationship with ourselves but also with the world around us.

The Light Breath

The following breathing technique allows you to amplify the life force energy flowing through your body. By combining the elements of light and breath, this practice delivers the energy needed to nurture and support you, reminding you of your inherent value and significance.

After doing this exercise, you may notice that you breathe more deeply throughout the day. Your body feels stronger with fewer aches and pains. You have more energy, and your thinking is clearer. Instead of saying, "Oh, god, another day, and I'm still here!" you get out of bed with joy in your heart.

You can use this technique every day. After a few sessions of conscious breathing, explore variations to find what works best for you. In this exercise, you'll take 50 breaths, shifting your focus after every ten. This will take about ten minutes. As you breathe, immerse yourself in the vibrant energy within each breath.

The first set of ten breaths:
As you settle into a comfortable position, take a moment to consciously relax. Focus your attention on your breathing. Count your breaths and pay attention to the rhythm with each inhale and exhale. You don't need to take deep breaths at this stage; the goal is to prepare for deeper, more nurturing inhalations.

The second set of ten breaths:
Breathing more deeply, imagine life-giving energy entering in the top of your head. Feel it flow down

through your body, arms, and legs, and out of your hands and feet. With intention, release any stuck energies and allow them to pass through. Now, pause and envision your body flooded with light. Your essence is light. Embrace this sensation and let it enliven you.

The third set of ten breaths:
Inhale, receiving the light into any part of your body where you feel pain or discomfort. You're not directing the light; you're opening yourself to its energy, allowing the affected areas to absorb it freely. You are making the light available to your body, and the body knows what to do with it, just as it instinctively knows how to utilize oxygen. Take a moment to pause and feel your entire being transformed into pure white light. Feel its warmth and restorative energy.

The fourth set of ten breaths:
Take deep, rhythmic breaths, fully embracing each inhale and exhale. As you breathe, allow the light and oxygen to fill your mind, emotions, senses, past, and future with their energy. This will increase your oxygen levels and boost your energy, leaving you feeling refreshed and uplifted.

The fifth set of ten breaths:

Inhale slowly and deeply; fully immerse yourself in the I AM that I AM. Since 'that' is an all-inclusive word, you can substitute any word you like, such as saying, "I AM worthy," or "I AM sovereign." Let the energy surge through you with each inhalation. Now, draw in the richness of I Matter, allowing it to permeate your being. Finally, breathe in the profound truth I EXIST, letting this energy resonate within you. As you breathe and repeat each of these statements, receive their vitality.

This practice takes about ten minutes. If you wake up during the night, use it to help you relax and drift back to sleep. You might find yourself dozing off before you finish. By focusing on conscious breathing, your mind cannot dwell on problems.

If you are tired and don't feel like practicing mindful breathing, remember that breath is life. Each breath you take enhances your body's light and oxygen levels, bringing in energy that can lift your mood and fill you with a sense of vitality. Conscious breathing reminds us of the joy of embodiment; it says yes to life.

Throughout the day, take a moment to stop and breathe slowly and deeply several times. This will reset your system, helping you feel more centered and calm.

By honoring your body this way, you harness a life-giving energy that can profoundly enhance your well-being.

So, the next time you question your worth, remember to take a deep breath. Then, feel the profound truth in these two simple words: I Matter.

Master Now - Rock Layout Badlands, SD

Support Tools

In My Soul I Am Free, Twitchell, Paul. 1968.

Peace Pilgrim: Her Life and Work in Her Own Words, Peace Pilgrim, 2013, Oceantree Books, Santa Fe, NM.

The Holographic Universe, Talbot, Michael, 1991, Harper Collins Publishers, New York, NY.

Way of the Peaceful Warrior: A Book that Changes Lives, Millman, Dan. 2006, New World Library.

Zero Limits, Hooponopono, Vitale, Joe. 2007, John Wiley & Sons. Hoboken, NJ.

Recommended Videos and Websites
    The Celestine Prophecy
    The Dark Crystal
    The Matrix
    What the Bleep Do We Know?
    Abraham-Hicks.com
    PmhAtwater.com

About the Author

Nancy DeYoung began a serious study of esoteric teachings in 1971, after being given the book *In My Soul I Am Free* by Paul Twitchell. Over the next two decades, she immersed herself in his works and then traveled for twenty years putting into practice what she learned. These experiences not only deepened her understanding but also inspired her to develop quantum shamanism. Her insights led to the publication of her book, *Modern Shamans: Own Your Wisdom*, which empowers the reader to embrace their innate wisdom and transformative potential.

Nancy says, "My books reflect my truth during different chapters of my life, each one a snapshot of my evolving perspective. They remind me that there is always another step to take on this journey of self-discovery."

Ms. DeYoung's books are available in bookstores and through online platforms like Amazon. They are available in both paperback and e-book formats, making them accessible to anyone ready to embark on their journey of transformation.

Modern Shamans: Own Your Wisdom
The Girl in the Tent: Memoir from the Road
Not My Dog

www.ingramcontent.com/pod-product-compliance
Lightning Source LLC
Chambersburg PA
CBHW021141090426
42740CB00008B/889